D0061830

dare to discipline

dare to discipline

JAMES DOBSON PH.D.

Co-published by

Tyndale House, Publishers, Wheaton, Illinois

Regal Books, G/L Publications, Glendale, California

Tenth printing, June 1974

Library of Congress Catalog Number 75-123283
SBN No. 8423-0630-7

Printed in the United States of America

To Danae, and her mother Shirley, I
affectionately dedicate the pages of this book
and the remaining years of my life.

Contents

Foreword

Everyone who has to do with children or youth should welcome this sound, straightforward, plainly written discussion of the ways in which order can be maintained, responsibility developed, and character built. It is a statement that has been long needed, on a subject that has been so much confused. Love is not enough. Discipline is not merely punishment. Good citizens cannot be produced in homes where children have good reason not to respect their own parents.

Successful education should be based on the psychological laws of learning, so often disregarded. Children learn to follow patterns that produce satisfactory results (to them). Good discipline is brought about by the intelligent application of this principle of reinforcement, although many parents consistently reinforce the behavior they want to eliminate. Dr. Dobson presents these principles and many others in a very readable style with abundant illustrations of good and bad "techniques."

He insists that the individual differences in natural endowment, and in social and emotional maturity must be considered in academic matters, and warns parents against expecting too much too soon.

One extremely valuable chapter tells how these principles can be applied effectively in the schools; another deals with creating effective moral behavior; still another is devoted entirely to the abuse of drugs.

Mother and father both get full attention and they are warned that they must show respect for their children if they want their children to show respect in return.

Dr. Dobson has had wide experience both as a teacher and as a psychologist. He makes technical procedures not merely understandable but interesting and often humorous. Best of all, readers who follow him will find that they get the results they want.

PAUL POPENOE, Sc. D., *Founder and President*
American Institute of Family Relations,
Los Angeles, California

Introduction

A mother recently asked for help in handling her defiant three-year-old daughter, Sandy. She had realized that her tiny little girl had hopelessly beaten her in a conflict of wills, and the child had become a tyrant and a dictator. On the afternoon prior to our conversation, an incident occurred which was typical of Sandy's way of doing business: the mother (I'll call her Mrs. Nichols) put the youngster down for a nap, although it was unlikely that she would stay in bed. Sandy is not accustomed to doing anything she doesn't want to do, and naptime is not on her acceptable list at the moment. On this occasion, however, the child was more interested in antagonizing her mom than in merely having her own way. Sandy began to scream. She yelled loudly enough to upset the whole neighborhood, fraying Mrs. Nichols' jangled nerves. Then she tearfully demanded various things, including a glass of water. At first Mrs. Nichols refused to comply with the orders, but she surrendered when Sandy's screaming again reached a peak of intensity. As the glass of water was delivered, the little tigress pushed it aside, refusing to drink because her mother had not brought it soon enough. Mrs. Nichols stood offering the water for a few minutes, then said she would take it back to the kitchen if Sandy did not drink by the time she counted to five. Sandy set her jaw and waited through the count. ". . . three, four, five!" As Mrs. Nichols grasped the glass and walked toward the kitchen, the child again screamed for water. Sandy dangled her harassed mom back and forth like a yo-yo until she tired of the sport.

Mrs. Nichols and her little daughter are among the many

casualties of an unworkable, illogical philosophy of child management which has dominated the literature on this subject during the past twenty years. This mother had read that a child will eventually respond to patience and tolerance, ruling out the need for discipline. She had been told to encourage the child's rebellion because it offered a valuable release of hostility. She attempted to implement the recommendation of the experts who suggested that she verbalize the child's feelings in a moment of conflict: "You want the water but you're angry because I brought it too late"; "You don't want me to take the water back to the kitchen"; "You don't like me because I make you take naps"; "You wish you could flush mommie down the toilet." She has been taught that conflicts between parent and child were to be perceived as inevitable misunderstandings or differences in viewpoint. Unfortunately, Mrs. Nichols and her advisors were wrong! She and her child were involved in no simple difference of opinion; she was being challenged, mocked, and defied by her daughter. No heart-to-heart talk would resolve this nose-to-nose confrontation, because the real issue was totally unrelated to the water or the nap or other aspects of the particular circumstances. The actual meaning behind this conflict and a hundred others was simply this: Sandy was brazenly rejecting the authority of her mother. The way Mrs. Nichols handled this confrontation would determine the nature of their future relationship; she could not ignore it. To quote the dilemma posed by a television commercial, "What's a mother to do?"

Much has been written about the dangers of harsh, oppressive, unloving discipline; these warnings are valid and should be heeded. However, the consequences of excessive punishment have been cited as justification for the elimination of discipline. That is foolish. There are times when a stiff-necked child will clench his little fists and dare his parent to accept his challenge; he is not motivated by frustration or inner hostility, as is often supposed. He merely wants to know where the boundaries lie and who's available to enforce them. Many well-meaning specialists have waved the banner of tolerance, but offered no solution for defiance. They have stressed the importance of parental understanding of the child, and I concur, but we need to teach Junior that he has a few things to learn about mamma, too. Mrs. Nichols and all her contemporaries need to know when to punish, how to set limits, and what behavior to inhibit. This disciplinary activity must occur within the framework of love and affection, which is often difficult for the parent who views these roles as contradictory. *Dare to Discipline* is addressed, in part, to this vital aspect of raising healthy, respectful children.

The term "discipline" is not limited to the context of punishment, and neither is this book. Children also need to be taught *self*-discipline and responsible behavior. They need assistance in learning how to face the challenge and obligations of living. They must learn the art of self-control. They should be equipped with the personal strength needed to meet the demands imposed on them by their school, peer group, and later adult responsibilities. There are those who believe these characteristics cannot be taught — that the best we can do is send the child down the path of least resistance, sweeping aside the hurdles during his formative years. The advocates of this laissez-faire philosophy would recommend that a child be allowed to fail in school if he chooses — or maintain his bedroom like the proverbial pigpen — or let his puppy go hungry. I reject this notion, and have accumulated considerable evidence to refute it. Children thrive best in an atmosphere of genuine love, undergirded by reasonable, consistent discipline. In a day of widespread drug usage, immorality, civil disobedience, vandalism, and violence, we must not depend on hope and luck to fashion the critical attitudes we value in our children. That unstructured technique was applied during the childhood of the generation which is now in college, and the outcome has been quite discouraging. Permissiveness has not just been a failure; it's been a disaster!

The recommendations in this manuscript are not experimental or speculative. They represent an approach to child management which can be trusted. They are not based on abstruse theoretical assumptions, but rather on practical consequences. As Jack London has stated, "The best measurement of anything should be: does it work?" When properly applied, discipline works! It permits the tender affection made possible by *mutual* respect between a parent and child. It bridges the generation gap which otherwise separates family members who should love and trust each other. It allows the God of our fathers to be introduced to our beloved children. It permits a teacher to do the kind of job in the classroom for which she is commissioned. It encourages a child to respect his fellowman, and live as a responsible, constructive citizen. As might be expected, there is a price tag on these benefits: they require courage, consistency, conviction, diligence, and enthusiastic effort. In short, one must *dare to discipline*.

I

Teaching Respect and Responsibility to Children

Nature has generously equipped most animals with a fear of things that could be harmful to them. Their survival depends on recognition of a particular danger in time to avoid it. But good old mother nature did not protect the frog quite so well; she overlooked a serious flaw in his early warning system that sometimes proves fatal. If a frog is placed in a pan of warm water under which the heat is being increased very gradually, he will typically show no inclination to escape. Since he is a cold-blooded creature, his body temperature remains approximately the same as the water around him and he does not notice the slow change taking place. As the temperature continues to intensify, the frog remains oblivious to his danger; he could easily hop his way to safety, but he is apparently thinking about something else. He will just sit there, contentedly peering over the edge of the pan while the steam curls ominously around his nostrils. Eventually, the boiling frog will pass on to his reward, having succumbed to an unnecessary misfortune that he could easily have avoided.

Now obviously, this is a book about parents and children,

not frogs. But human beings have some of the same per-
ceptual inadequacies as their little green friends. We quickly become excited about *sudden* dangers that confront us.
War, disease epidemics, earthquakes, and hurricanes bring
instant mobilization. However, if a threatening problem
arises very slowly, perhaps over a decade or two, we often
allow ourselves to "boil" in happy ignorance. This blind-
ness to gradual disasters is best illustrated by the way we
have ignored the turmoil that is spreading systematically
through the younger generation of Americans. We have
passively accepted a slowly deteriorating "youth scene"
without uttering a croak of protest. Suppose the parents of
yesterday could make a brief visit to our world to observe
the conditions that prevail among our children; certainly,
they would be dismayed and appalled by the juvenile
problems which have been permitted to become widespread
(and are spreading wider) in urban America.

Narcotic and drug usage by America's juveniles is an in-
describable shame. Although the danger is now getting wide
publicity, the adult who has not worked with teen-agers recently may be unaware of the degree to which this activity
has infiltrated adolescent society in the past few years. In
1960 there were 1,500 juvenile arrests for narcotics usage
in the State of California; in 1968 there were 30,000. That
is an increase of 2,000 percent in an eight-year period. The
magnitude of the problem was further described in the
following quotation, taken from a recent article in *Time*
magazine:

> "A heroin epidemic has hit us. We must face that
> fact," says Dr. Donald Louria, president of the New
> York State Council on Drug Addiction and author of
> *Drug Scene.* Dr. Elliot Luby, associate director of De-
> troit's addict-treating Lafayette Clinic, concurs: "Addic-
> tion is really reaching epidemic proportions. You have
> to look at it as an infectious disease." Epidemic, of

course, is a relative term, but as a Chicago psychiatrist, Dr. Marvin Schwarz, says: "Now we're seeing it clinically, whereas before we weren't. The kids on heroin all have long histories of drug use." At the California-based Synanon self-help centers for addicts, the teen-age population has risen from zero five years ago to 400 today. In San Francisco, Dr. Barry Ramer, director of the Study for Special Problems, calls heroin now "the most readily available drug on the streets." He adds: "In my wildest nightmares, I never dreamed of what we are seeing today."*

Many young people are now playing another dangerous game, packaged neatly under the title of sexual freedom. The rationale sounds very plausible: why should you be restricted by the hangups of the past generation? Why shouldn't you enjoy this greatest of life's pleasures? Now that God is dead, who has the authority to deny you this fulfillment? Contraceptives will prevent babies, so why not find out what everyone is talking about? Now certainly, illicit sex is not a new phenomenon; this activity has been with us for a few thousand years. However, immorality has never been embraced as right and proper in America until now. "Bed today, wed tomorrow — maybe" is the plea. Without being unnecessarily pessimistic, it is accurate to say that the traditional concept of morality is *dead* among the majority of high school students today. The "Playboy Philosophy" has been accepted as the banner of the now generation. I spoke recently to a group of high school homemaking teachers who related their surprise at the blatant admission of immorality by their students. Whole classes now argue with their teachers about the "rightness" of sexual freedom.

The casualties of this permissive sexual philosophy have

Time magazine, March 16, 1970, p. 16. Used by permission.

been known for centuries and can hardly be overlooked today: (1) illegitimate pregnancies and their accompanying heartache are common in most high schools in this country. (2) Venereal disease has reached epidemic proportions within the cities. A physician who directs a venereal disease clinic recently described for me the depressing conditions he witnesses. He said most of his young patients do not come wringing their hands in despair at the awful disease they have contracted; rather, they schedule routine visits to his clinic in order to "cure" what they carry in time for the events of the next weekend! The medical examination serves as a pit stop for their upcoming exploits. (3) Perhaps the most severe result of promiscuity is the effect it has on the emotions and personality, subjecting innocence and wholesomeness to an untimely death. These consequences of sexual permissiveness are not widely advertised by the advocates of the new morality!

Another symptom of the adolescent unrest is seen in the frequent display of aggression and hostility. Young people are more violent today than at any period in American history. According to published FBI figures, juvenile arrests for aggravated assault have increased seventy percent faster than the general population in recent years. Two-thirds of all the crimes of violence (murder, rape, and assault) are committed by those under twenty-one years of age. A recent Associated Press article stated that students across the United States are attacking their teachers with increasing frequency. Most of these physical attacks occur in the junior and senior high schools, although a surprising number of the episodes take place at the elementary school level. Can there be any doubt that school authority is being challenged seriously?

There are many related phenomena occurring among the young which reveal the turmoil in adolescent society. Emotional maladjustment, gang warfare, teen-age suicide, school failure, shoplifting, and grand larceny are symptoms of a deeper illness that plague vast numbers of America's young. During the earlier days of the adolescent rebellion, the reassuring watchword was "only a small percentage of the youngsters are getting into trouble." That statement no longer comforts us, because it is no longer true. On the other hand, it would be grossly unfair to say that most young people are "bad"; they are merely responding to social forces and causes that are leading them into the icy face of disaster.

We cannot solve these problems by lashing out at the young with venom and hostility. Many of the youngsters who are behaving in such antisocial and self-destructive ways are actually lost, aimless and valueless individuals. Millions of other teen-agers have not attacked society or rejected its time-honored values, yet they experience the same inner emptiness and confusion. They are badly in need of wise and understanding parents who can anchor them during their personal crises. Certainly, the purpose of this book is not to condemn our children; they are our most important and valued resource. To the contrary, the older generation must assume the blame for allowing the circumstances to deteriorate. There was a time when the trend could easily have been reversed, but like the contented frog, we must have been thinking about something else. The time has come for us to hop, rather than boil. It is our parental responsibility to get off our corpulent behinds and take steps to eliminate the problems which threaten our children. We may not salvage some members of the present generation but perhaps we can preserve the next. Ultimately, we must deal with this question: how did we get into this mess and how can we get out of it?

Without meaning to oversimplify a very complicated pic-

ture, it is accurate to say that many of our difficulties with
the present generation of young people began in the tender
years of their childhood. Little children are exceedingly
vulnerable to the teaching (good or bad) of their guardians,
and mistakes made in the early years prove costly, indeed.
There is a critical period during the first four or five years
of a child's life when he can be taught proper attitudes.
These early concepts become rather permanent. When the
opportunity of those years is missed, however, the prime
receptivity usually vanishes, never to return. If it is desirable that children be kind, appreciative, and pleasant, those
qualities should be taught — not hoped for. If we want to
see honesty, truthfulness, and unselfishness in our offspring,
then these characteristics should be the conscious objectives
of our early instructional process. If it is important to produce respectful, responsible young citizens, then we should
set out to mold them accordingly. The point is obvious:
*heredity does not equip a child with proper attitudes; chil-
dren will learn what they are taught.* We cannot expect the
desirable attitudes and behavior to appear if we have not
done our early homework. It seems clear that many of the
parents of the post-war crop of American babies failed in
that critical assignment.

Nature is rather careless about whom it allows to become
mammas and papas. The qualifications are not very high;
in fact, it is not necessary to know a single fact about children in order to produce one. Young men and women may
find themselves saddled with the unwanted responsibility for
impressionable, helpless infants, about whom they know
nothing. They may be totally ignorant of the principles of
discipline, nutrition, or child growth and development. The
mistakes that they make are certainly unintentional, yet
the consequences are no less severe. Perhaps the greatest
and most common shortcoming during the past twenty-five

years was related to the belief, particularly by new parents, that "love is enough" in raising children. Apparently they believed that successful parenthood consists of two primary obligations: (1) raise the child in an atmosphere of genuine affection; (2) satisfy his material and physical needs. They expected every good and worthwhile virtue to bubble forth from this spring of lovingkindness. As time has shown, that was wishful thinking. Although love is essential to human life, parental responsibility extends far beyond it. A parent may love a child immeasurably, and then proceed to teach him harmful attitudes. Love in the absence of instruction will not produce a child with self-discipline, self-control, and respect for his fellow man. Affection and warmth underlie all mental and physical health, yet they do not eliminate the need for careful training and guidance.

At a recent psychologists' conference in Los Angeles, the keynote speaker made the statement that *the greatest social disaster of this century is the belief that abundant love makes discipline unnecessary*. He said that some of the little terrors who are unmanageable in the school classroom are *mistakenly* believed to have emotional problems. They are referred to the school psychologist for his evaluation of their difficulty, but no deep problems are found. Instead, it becomes obvious that the children have simply never been required to inhibit their behavior or restrict their impulses. Some of these children came from homes where love was almost limitless.

Respectful and responsible children result from families where the proper combination of *love and discipline* is present. Both these ingredients must be applied in the necessary quantities. An absence of either is often disastrous. During the 1950s, an unfortunate imbalance existed, when we saw the predominance of a happy theory called "permissive democracy." This philosophy minimized parental

obligations to control their children, in some cases making
mom and dad feel that all forms of punishment were harmful and unfair. As a result, the mid-century decade has
been described as the most permissive ten years in our history. Is it merely coincidental that the generation raised
during that era has grown up to challenge every form of
authority that confronts it? I think not. It should come as
no surprise that our beloved children have hangups; we
have sacrificed this generation on the altar of overindul-
gence, permissiveness, and smother-love. Certainly, other
factors have contributed to the present unsettled youth
scene, but I believe the major cause has been related to the
anarchy that existed in millions of American homes.

Have you considered the fact that the present generation
of young people has enjoyed more of the "good life" than
any comparable group in the history of the world? One can
define the good life any way he chooses; the conclusion remains the same. Our children have had more pleasure and
entertainment, better food, more leisure time, better education, better medicine, more material goods, and more opportunities than has ever been known before. Yet they
have been described as the "angry generation." How can
this be? Those two conditions do not seem to fit together.
Down through the ages, people have dreamed and longed
for a day when their major troubles would be resolved: "If
we just didn't have this terrible war to fight; if we could
eliminate this famine, or this depression, or this plague."
At last in post-war America, 1950-1970, a generation was
born on which all the coveted goodness was heaped. But
instead of bringing exuberance and gratitude, there has
come antagonism and haughty contempt for the generation
that worked to provide it. Why? Most of the popular answers are essentially wrong. The conflict has not occurred
because of hypocrisy in the older generation. There has al-

ways been hypocrisy in human society and it is certainly well represented in ours. But if hypocrisy is the root-cause of the turmoil, why didn't previous generations respond as violently? Something else is operating now. Likewise, the problem has not resulted from the existence of the H-bomb or from restriction on free speech or from poverty or from racial injustice. Without question, all of these factors have had their impact on society, but the central cause of the turmoil among the young must again be found in the tender years of childhood: we demanded neither respect nor responsible behavior from our children, and it should not be surprising that some of our young citizens are now demonstrating the absence of these virtues.

A SHORT ESSAY ON CHILD DISCIPLINE

Methods and philosophies regarding control of children have been the subject of heated debate and disagreement for centuries. The pendulum has swept back and forth regularly between harsh, oppressive discipline and the unstructured permissiveness of the 1950s. It is time that we realize that *both* extremes leave their characteristic scars on the lives of young victims, and I would be hard pressed to say which is more damaging. Unfortunately, the prevailing philosophy at a particular time seems to be more influential on parental approaches to discipline than does common sense. For example, I know of one mother who spanks her six-month-old baby for not lying still while being diapered. Many such foolish examples of repressive discipline are easily observable in our society. However, the opposite is still more prevalent. I knew of a family with four of the world's most undisciplined children. These youngsters were the terrors of their neighborhood; they were disrespectful, loud, and aggressive. They roamed in and out of garages, helping themselves to tools and equipment. It became necessary for neighbors to remove the handles from outside water faucets, because these children enjoyed leaving the water running when the families were gone. It was interesting to observe the method of discipline used by their mother, because whatever it was, it didn't work. Her system of controlling children boiled down to a simple formula: she would rush out the front door about once every hour, and scream: "I have just had it with you; I have had it with you kids!" Then she would turn and go back into the house. The children never even looked up at her. If they knew she was there they gave no indication of it. She apparently felt it was sufficient for her to come out like a cuckoo clock and remind them that she was still on the job. Certainly, it is not difficult to find such classic examples of poor discipline. Logical, reasonable, and consistent approaches to discipline are a bit more rare.

The American public has been subjected to many wildhorse opinions about child discipline, which have galloped off rapidly in all directions. Everyone from Aunt Bessie to the local undertaker has his own unique viewpoint about how children should be controlled, and what is worse, the experts have often been in direct contradiction with one another. The cause of their disagreement is simple: the principles of good discipline cannot be ascertained by scientific inquiry. The subject is too complicated and there are too many variables involved. Psychologists have been criticized and even ridiculed because they could not agree on a workable philosophy of child mangement, and yet every other profession has its unresolvable conflicts as well. The Supreme Court often splits five to four in its interpretation of the law. Physicians disagree violently on hundreds of medical issues, although their patients are usually unaware that the controversy exists. Likewise, there are thorny, unsettled questions to be faced by every profession and it should not be considered strange that experts on the subject of child development have failed to agree on the ideal approach to discipline in the home. Despite this disagreement in the past, I am thoroughly convinced that the proper control of children can be found in a reasonable, common sense philosophy, where five key elements are paramount.

1. Developing respect for the parents is the critical factor in child management

It is most important that a child respect his parents, not for the purpose of satisfying their egos, but because the child's relationship with his parents provides the basis for his attitude toward all other people. His view of parental authority becomes the cornerstone of his later outlook on school authority, police and law, the people with whom he will eventually live and work, and for society in general. The parent-child relationship is the first and most important social interaction an infant will have, and the flaws and knots in that interaction can often be seen in later relationships. For example, suppose a child wants some candy but his parents refuse, so he falls down on the floor and screams and bangs his head on the carpet. Mamma then becomes upset by the display and says, "Here, Johnny, I guess one piece of candy won't hurt you. Now stop crying." She has made it profitable for Johnny to react emotionally. His yelling paid a tasty dividend. He challenged the system and won the battle. If good-hearted mom follows that same approach to his protests during the next fourteen years, little Johnny may gradually grow up to become Big Bad John, expecting everyone else to yield to his demands as his

weak old mamma did. When rebuffed later by a less pliable
authority, the stage is set for a violent collision. Although
this example is deliberately oversimplified, I could give
many similar illustrations which would show how the early
parent-child relationship is reflected in later human interaction.

Respect for the parent must be maintained for another
equally important reason. If you want your child to accept
your values when he reaches his teen years, then you must
be worthy of his respect during his younger days. When a
child can successfully defy his parents during his first fifteen
years, laughing in their faces and stubbornly flouting their
authority, he develops a natural contempt for them. "Stupid
old Mom and Dad! I've got them wound around my little
finger. Sure they love me, but I really think they're afraid of
me." A child may not utter these words, but he feels them
each time he outsmarts his adult companions and wins the
confrontations and battles. Later he is likely to demonstrate
his disrespect in a more open manner. His parents are not
deserving of his respect, and he does not want to identify
with anything they represent. He rejects every vestige of
their philosophy. This factor is important for Christian
parents who wish to sell their concept of God to their children.
They must first sell themselves. If they are not
worthy of respect, then neither is their religion or their
morals, or their government, or their country, or any of their
values. This becomes the "generation gap" at its most basic
level. The chasm does not develop from a failure to communicate;
we're speaking approximately the same language.
Mark Twain once said about the Bible, "It's not the things
I don't understand that bother me; it's the things I do!"
Likewise, our difficulties between generations result more
from what we *do* understand in our communication than in
our confusion with words. The conflict between generations

occurs because of a breakdown in mutual respect, and it bears many painful consequences.

The issue of respect can be a useful tool in knowing when to punish and how excited one should get about a given behavior. First, the parent should decide whether an undesirable behavior represents a direct challenge of his authority — to his position as the father or mother. Punishment should depend on that evaluation. For example, suppose little Walter is acting silly in the living room, and he falls into a table, breaking many expensive china cups and other trinkets. Or suppose he loses his bicycle or leaves Dad's best saw out in the rain. These are acts of childish irresponsibility and should be handled as such. Perhaps the parent should have the child work to pay for the losses — depending on the age and maturity of the child, of course. However, these examples do not constitute direct challenges to authority. They do not emanate from willful, haughty disobedience. In my opinion, spankings should be reserved for the moment a child (age ten or less) expresses a defiant "I will not!" or "You shut up!" When a youngster tries this kind of stiff-necked rebellion, you had better take it out of him, and pain is a marvelous purifier. When nose-to-nose confrontation occurs between you and your child, it is not the time to have a discussion about the virtues of obedience. It is not the occasion to send him in his room to pout. It is not appropriate to wait until poor, tired old dad comes plodding in from work, just in time to handle the conflicts of the day. You have drawn a line in the dirt, and the child has deliberately flopped his big hairy toe across it. Who is going to win? Who has the most courage? Who is in charge here? If you do not answer these questions conclusively for the child, he will precipitate other battles designed to ask them again and again. It is the ultimate paradox of childhood that a youngster wants to be controlled, but he insists that his parents earn the right to control him.

Mr. Holloway was the father of a teen-age girl named Becky. He came to see me in desperation one afternoon and related the cause for this concern. Becky had never been required to obey or respect her parents, and her early years were hectic for the entire family. Mrs. Holloway was confident that Becky would eventually become more manageable, but that improvement never came. This child held her parents in utter contempt from her youngest childhood. She was sullen, disrespectful, selfish, and uncooperative. Mr. and Mrs. Holloway did not feel they had the right to make demands on their daughter, so they smiled politely and pretended not to notice. Their magnanimous attitude became more difficult to maintain as Becky steamrolled into puberty and adolescence. She was a perpetual malcontent, sneering at her family in disgust. Mr. and Mrs. Holloway were afraid to antagonize her in any way because she would throw the most violent tantrums imaginable. They were victims of emotional blackmail. They thought they could buy her cooperation, which led them to install a private telephone in her room. She accepted it without gratitude and accumulated an $86.00 bill during the first month of usage. They thought a party might make her happy. Mrs. Holloway worked very hard to get the house decorated and the refreshments prepared. On the appointed evening, a mob of dirty, profane teen-agers swarmed into the house, breaking and destroying the furnishings as they came. During the course of the evening, Mrs. Holloway said something that angered Becky. Mr. Holloway had been away from home, and he returned to find his wife lying in a pool of blood in the bathroom. Becky had struck her down and left her helpless on the floor; he found his unconcerned daughter in the backyard, dancing with her friends. He spoke with tears in his eyes as he described for me the details of their private nightmare. Mrs. Holloway was still in the hospital contemplating her parental failures. The greatest tragedy in this incident lies in the permanence of the problem; no simple therapy can eradicate the scars that are burned into the lives of these three unfortunate people. They have paid an exorbitant price for underestimating the importance of respect in Becky's early childhood.

Much sound advice has been written about the dangers of inappropriate discipline, and it should be heeded. A parent can absolutely destroy a child through the application of harsh, oppressive, whimsical, unloving, and/or capricious punishment. I am certainly not recommending such. However, you cannot inflict permanent damage to a child if you follow this technique: identify the rules well in advance; let there be no doubt about what is and is not acceptable behavior; when the child cold-bloodedly chooses to challenge those known boundaries in a haughty manner, give him good reason to regret it; at all times, demonstrate love and affection and kindness and understanding. *Discipline and love are not antithetical*; one is a function of the other. The parent must convince himself that punishment (as outlined above) is not something he does *to* the child; it is something he does *for* the child. His attitude towards his disobedient youngster is this, "I love you too much to let you behave like that." For the small child, an illustration can carry the message most clearly:

I knew of a little birdie who was in his nest with his mommie. The mommie bird went off to find some worms to eat, and she told the little bird not to get out of the nest while she was gone. But the little bird didn't mind her, and he jumped out of the nest and fell to the ground where a big cat got him. When I tell you to mind me, it is because I know what is best for you, just as the mother bird did with the little birdie. When I tell you to stay in the front yard, it's because I don't want you to run in the street and get hit by a car. I love you and I don't want anything to happen to you. If you don't mind me, I'll have to spank you to help you remember how important it is. Do you understand?

My own mother had an unusual understanding of good disciplinary procedures. She was very tolerant of my childishness, and I found her reasonable on most issues. If I was late coming home from school, I could just explain what had caused the delay, and that was the end of the matter. If I didn't get my work done, we could sit down and come to some kind of agreement for future action. But there was one matter on which she was absolutely rigid: she did not tolerate "sassiness." She knew that backtalk and "lip" are the child's most potent weapons of defiance and they must be discouraged. I learned very early that if I was going to launch a flippant attack on her, I had better be standing at least ten or twelve feet away. This distance was necessary to avoid being hit with whatever she could get in her hands. On one occasion she cracked me with a shoe; at other times she used a handy belt. The day I learned the importance of staying out of reach shines like a neon light in my mind. I made the costly mistake of "sassing" her when I was about four feet away. She wheeled around to grab something with which to hit me, and her hand landed on a girdle. She drew back and swung that abominable garment in my direction, and I can still hear it whistling through the air. The intended blow caught me across the chest, followed by a multitude of straps and buckles, wrapping themselves around my mid-section. She gave me an entire thrashing with one massive blow! From that day forward, I cautiously retreated a few steps before popping off.

Respect is unsuccessful as a unilateral affair; it must

operate on a *two-way* street. A mother cannot require her child to treat her with dignity if she will not do the same for him. She should be gentle with his ego, never belittling him or embarrassing him in front of his friends. Punishment should usually be administered away from the curious eyes of gloating onlookers. The child should not be laughed at unmercifully. His strong feelings and requests, even if foolish, should be given an honest appraisal. He should feel that his parents "really *do* care about me." Self-esteem is the most fragile attribute in human nature; it can be damaged by a very minor incident and its reconstruction is often difficult to engineer. A father who is sarcastic and biting in his criticism of children cannot expect to receive genuine respect in return. His offspring might *fear* him enough to conceal their contempt, but revenge will often erupt in late adolescence. Children know the wisdom of the old axiom which recommends, "Don't mock the alligator until you are across the stream." Thus, a vicious, toothy father may intimidate his household for a time, but if he does not demonstrate respect for its inhabitants, they may return his hostility when they reach the safety of early adulthood.

A mother can expect her child to challenge her authority regularly from the time he is about fifteen months of age, if not earlier. The toddler is the world's most hard-nosed opponent of law and order, and he can make life miserable for his harassed mom. In his own innocent way, he is vicious and selfish and demanding and cunning and destructive. Comedian Bill Cosby must have had some personal losses at the hands of a toddler; he is quoted as saying, "Give me 200 active two-year-olds and I can conquer the world." The child between fifteen and thirty months of age does not want to be restricted or inhibited in any manner and he is not inclined to conceal his viewpoint. He resents every nap imposed on him, and bedtime becomes an exhausting

ordeal to be dreaded. He wants to play with everything he
sees, particularly fragile and expensive ornaments. He prefers using his pants rather than the potty, and he insists on
eating with his hands. When he breaks loose in a store, he
invariably runs as fast as his fat little legs will carry him.
He picks up the kitty by her ears, and then screams in
protest when he gets scratched. He wants his mamma to be
within three feet of him all day long, preferably serving as
his full-time playmate. Truly, the toddler is a tiger! Even
if his parents do everything right in disciplining him, they
are still likely to find him hard to control. For this reason,
they should not hope to make their two-year-old act like an
adult. A controlling but patient hand will eventually succeed in settling the little tyrant, but probably not until he is
about four years of age. Unfortunately, however, the child's
attitude toward authority can be severely damaged during
his toddler years. The parent who loves her cute little but-
terball so much that she cannot risk antagonizing him, may
lose and never regain his control.

I dealt with the mother of a rebellious thirteen-year-old
who was totally beyond her parental authority. He would
not come home at night until 2:00 A.M. or later and he deliberately disobeyed every request she made of him. I asked
if she could tell me the history of this problem, since I correctly assumed that her lack of control was a long-standing
difficulty. She said she clearly remembered where it all
started. Her son was less than three years old at the time.
She carried him to his room and placed him in his crib,
and he spit in her face to demonstrate his usual bedtime
attitude. She attempted to explain the importance of not
spitting in mommie's face, but her lecture was interrupted
by another moist missile. This mother had been told that
all confrontation could be resolved by love and understanding and discussion. She wiped her face and began

again, at which point the youngster hit her with another well-aimed blast. She began to get frustrated by this time, and she shook him, but not hard enough to throw off his aim for the next contribution. What could she do then? Her philosophy offered no honorable solution to this embarrassing challenge. Finally, she rushed from the room in utter exasperation, and her little conquerer spat on the back of the door as it shut. She lost; he won! She said she never had the upper hand with her child after that night!

When a parent loses the early confrontations with the child, the later conflicts become harder to win. The parent who never wins, who is too weak or too tired or too busy to win, is making a costly mistake that will come back to haunt him during the child's adolescence. If you can't make a five-year-old pick up his toys, it is unlikely that you will exercise any impressive degree of control during his adolescence, the most defiant time of life. It is important to understand that adolescence is a condensation or composite of all the training and behavior that has gone before. Any unsettled matter in the first twelve years is likely to fester and erupt during adolescence. The proper time to begin disarming the teen-age time-bomb is twelve years before it arrives. Perhaps the most difficult problems referred to me occur with the rebellious, hostile teen-ager for whom the parents have done everything wrong since he was born. He hates them and they do not know why, because they love him thoroughly. Since adolescence is the age of natural rebellion, antagonism is added to antagonism. His relationship with his parents has long since reached a solidified stage where change is unlikely. For a psychologist, this problem must be approached as a physician views terminal cancer: "I can't cure it now;

it's too late. Perhaps I can make its consequences less painful."

I must point out the fact that some rebellious behavior is distinctly different in origin from the "challenging" defiance I've been describing. A child's antagonism and stiff-lipped negativism may emanate from frustration, disappointment, or rejection, and must be interpreted as a warning signal to be heeded. Perhaps the toughest task in parenthood is to recognize the difference between these two distinct motives. A child's resistant behavior always contains a message to his parents which they must decode before responding. That message is often phrased in the form of a question: "Are you in charge or am I?" A forceful reply is appropriate to that query as a discouragement to his future attempts to overthrow constituted government in the home. On the other hand, Junior's antagonism may be saying, "I feel unloved now that I'm stuck with that yelling baby brother. Mom used to care for me; now nobody wants me. I hate everybody." When this kind of meaning underlies the rebellion, the parents should move quickly to pacify its cause. The most successful parents are those who have the skill to get behind the eyes of the child, seeing what he sees, thinking what he thinks, feeling what he feels. Unless they can master this ability, they will continually react in a harmful manner. For example, when a two-year-old screams and cries at bedtime, one must ascertain what he is communicating. If he is genuinely frightened by the blackness of his room, the appropriate response should be quite different than if he is merely protesting about having to go nighty-night. The art of good parenthood revolves around the interpretation of meaning behind behavior.

Repeating the first point, the most vital objective of disciplining a child is to gain and maintain his respect. If the parents fail in this task, life becomes complicated, indeed.

2. *The best opportunity to communicate often occurs after punishment*

Nothing brings a parent and child closer together than for the mother or father to win decisively after being defiantly challenged. This is particularly true if the child was "asking for it," knowing full well that he deserved what he got. The parent's demonstration of his authority builds respect like no other process, and the child will often reveal his affection when the emotion has passed. For this reason, the parent should not dread or shrink back from these confrontations with the child. These occasions should be anticipated as important events, because they provide the opportunity to say something to the child that cannot be said at other times. It is not necessary to beat the child into submission; a little bit of pain goes a long way for a young child. However, the spanking should be of sufficient magnitude to cause the child to cry genuinely. After the emotional ventilation, the child will often want to crumple to the breast of his parent, and he should be welcomed with open, warm, loving arms. At that moment you can talk heart to heart. You can tell him how much you love him, and how important he is to you. You can explain why he was punished and how he can avoid the difficulty next time. This kind of communication is not made possible by other disciplinary measures, including standing the child in the corner or taking away his firetruck.

I was attempting to teach the art of good discipline to the mother of a fifteen-month-old girl, and she related an incident to me which illustrates the desired outcome. Suzie decided she didn't want to mind her mother, Mrs. Butler, when told not to run out the back door. It was sprinkling and Mrs. Butler did not want her to go outside because she was barefoot. Suzie's mother went out to get some firewood and told her to wait in the doorway. The child knew the meaning of the command because she learned to talk quite early; nevertheless, she came toddling across the patio. Mrs. Butler caught her and took her back, giving the same order more sternly. As soon as her back was turned, Suzie ran out again. On the third trip, her mother stung her little legs a few times with a switch. After the tears had subsided, Mrs. Butler was putting the firewood in the fireplace when Suzie came to her and reached out her arms, saying "Love, mommie." She gathered her child tenderly in her arms, of course, and rocked her for fifteen minutes, talking softly about the importance of obedience.

Parental warmth after punishment is essential to demonstrate to the child that it was his behavior, and not the child himself, that the parent rejected. William Glasser, the father of Reality Therapy, made this distinction very clear when he described the difference between discipline and punishment. "Discipline" is directed at the objectionable behavior, and the child will accept its consequences without resentment. By contrast, he defined punishment as a response that is directed at the individual. As such it is deeply resented by the child; punishment is the parent's personal thrust at the child; it is a desire of one person to hurt another; it is an expression of hostility rather than corrective love. When authorities talk about the emotional dangers of corporal punishment (spanking), they fail to discriminate between these two important approaches. Although Glasser's definition of the term punishment has not been applied throughout this book, the concept he has conveyed is of the greatest importance. Unquestionably, there is a wrong way to correct a child, and a major recurring error at this point can make a youngster feel unloved, unwanted, and insecure. One of the best guarantees against these misinterpretations is a loving conclusion to the disciplinary session.

3. *Control without nagging (It is possible)*

Yelling and nagging at children can become a habit, and an ineffectual one at that! Have you ever screamed at your child, "This is the last time I'm going to tell you, 'this is that last time' "? Parents often use anger to get action, instead of using action to get action. It doesn't work. Let me give you an example.

Eight-year-old Henry is sitting on the floor, playing with his games. Mom looks at her watch and says, "Henry, it's nearly nine o'clock (a thirty-minute exaggeration) so gather up your junk and go take your bath." Now Henry knows, and Mom knows, that she doesn't mean for him to go take a bath. She merely meant for him to start *thinking* about going to take his bath. She would have fainted dead away if he had responded to her empty command. Approximately ten minutes later, Mom speaks again, "Now, Henry, it is getting later and you have to go to school tomorrow, and I want those toys picked up; then go get in that tub!" She still does not intend for Henry to obey, and he knows it. Her *real* message is "We're getting closer, Hank." Henry shuffles around and stacks a box or two to demonstrate that he heard her. Then he settles down for a few more minutes of play. Six minutes pass, and Mom issues another command, this time with more passion and threat in her voice, "Now listen, young man, I told you to get a move on, and I meant it." To Henry, this means he must get his toys picked up and meander toward the bathroom door. If his mom pursues him with a rapid step, then he must carry out the assignment posthaste. However, if Mom's mind wanders before she performs the last step of this ritual, Henry is free to enjoy a few more seconds reprieve.

You see, Henry and his mom are involved in a one-act play; they both know the rules and the role being enacted by the opposite player. The entire scene is programmed, computerized, and scripted. Whenever Mom wants Henry to do something he dislikes, she progresses through graduated steps of phony anger, beginning with calm and ending with a red flush and a threat. Henry does not have to move until she reaches the peak anger point. How foolish this game is! Since Mom controls him by the use of empty threats she has to stay mad all the time. Her relationship with her children is contaminated, and she ends each day with a pounding, throbbing headache. She can never count on instant obedience; it takes her at least five minutes to work up a believeable degree of anger.

How much better it is to use *action* to get action. There are hundreds of tools which will bring the desired response, some of which involve pain while others offer the child a reward. The use of rewards (bribes) is discussed in the next chapter, and thus will not be presented here. But minor pain can also provide excellent motivation for the child. The parent should have some means of making the child want to cooperate, other than simply obeying because he was told to do so. For those who can think of no such device, I will suggest one: there is a muscle, lying snugly against the base of the neck. Anatomy books list it as the trapezius muscle, and when firmly squeezed, it sends little messengers to the brain saying, "This hurts; avoid recurrence at all costs." The pain is only temporary; it can cause no damage. When the youngster ignores being told to do something by his parent, he should know that Mom has a practical recourse. Let's return to the bedtime issue between Henry and his Mom; she should have told him that he had fifteen more minutes to play. It then would have been wise to set the alarm clock or the stove buzzer to sound in fifteen minutes. No one, child or adult, likes a sudden interruption to his activity. When the time came, Mom should have quietly told Henry to go take his bath. If he didn't move immediately, the shoulder muscle could have been squeezed. If Henry learns that this procedure is invariably followed, he will move before the consequence is applied.

There will be those among my readers who feel that the deliberate, premeditated application of minor pain to a sweet little child is a harsh and unloving recommendation. I ask those skeptics to hear me out. Consider the alternatives. On the one hand, there is constant nagging and strife between parent and child. When the youngster discovers there is no threat behind the millions of words he hears, he stops listening to them. The only messages he responds to are those reaching a peak of emotion, which means there is much screaming and yelling going on. The child is pulling in the opposite direction, fraying Mom's nerves and straining the parent-child relationship. But the most important limitation of these verbal reprimands is that their user often has to resort to physical punishment in the end, anyway. Thus, instead of the discipline being administered in a calm and judicious manner, the parent has become unnerved and frustrated, swinging wildly at the belligerent child. There was no reason for a fight to have occurred. The situation could have ended very differently if the parental attitude had been one of confident serenity. Speaking softly, almost pleasantly, Mom says, "Henry, you know what happens when you don't mind me; now I don't see any reason in the world why I should have to make you feel pain to get your cooperation tonight, but if you insist, I'll play the game with you. When the buzzer sounds you let me know what your decision is." The child has a choice to make, and the advantages to him of obeying his mother's wishes are clear. She need not scream. She need not threaten to shorten his life. She need not become upset. She is in command. Of course, Mother will have to prove two or three times that she will apply the pain, if necessary, and occasionally throughout the coming months her child will check to see if she is still at the helm. But there is no question in my mind as to which of these two approaches involves the least pain and the least hostility between parent and child.

The shoulder muscle is a surprisingly useful source of minor pain; actually, it was created expressly for school teachers. It can be utilized in those countless situations where face-to-face confrontations occur between adult and child. One such incident happened to me several years ago. I had come out of a drug store, and there at its entrance was a stooped, elderly man, approximately seventy-five or eighty years of age. Four boys, probably ninth graders, had cornered him and were running circles around him. As I came through the door, one of the boys had just knocked the man's hat down over his eyes and they were laughing about how silly he looked, leaning on his cane. I stepped in front of the poor fellow and suggested that the boys find someone else to torment. They called me names, and then sauntered off down the street. I got in my car, and was gone for about fifteen minutes. I returned to get something I had forgotten, and as I was getting out of my car, I saw the same four boys come running out of a nearby hardware store. The proprietor of the shop ran out after them, shaking his fist and screaming in protest. I discovered later that they had run down the rows in his store, raking cans and bottles off on the floor. They also made fun of the fact that he was Jewish and rather fat. When the boys saw me coming, I'm sure they thought I believed myself to be Robin Hood II, protector of the innocent and friend of the oppressed. One of the little tormentors ran straight up to my face, and stared defiantly in my eye. He was about half my size, but he obviously felt safe because he was a child. He said, "You just hit me! I'll sue you for everything you're worth." I have rather large hands, and it was obviously the time to use them; I grasped his shoulder muscles on both sides, squeezing firmly. He dropped to the ground, holding his neck. One of his friends said, "I'll bet you're a school teacher, aren't you?" All four of them ran. Later that evening I received a call from the police, saying that these four boys had harassed merchants and customers along that block for weeks. Their parents did not choose to cooperate with the authorities and the police did not know what to do about the assaults. I can think of no more excellent way to breed, cultivate, and finalize juvenile delinquency than to allow such examples of early defiance to succeed with impunity.

Discipline in a school classroom is not very different from discipline at home; the principles by which children can be controlled are the same in both settings — only the methods change. A teacher, scoutmaster, or recreation leader who tries to control a group of children by use of his own anger is due for a long, long day of frustration. The children find out how far he will go before taking any action, and they invariably push him right to that line. Perhaps the most nonsensical mistake a teacher or group leader can make is to impose disciplinary measures that the children do not dislike. I knew a teacher, for example, who

would scream and yell and beg her class to cooperate.
When they got completely out of hand, she resorted to her
maximum firepower: she would climb up on her desk and
blow her whistle! The kids loved it! She weighed about
240 pounds, and the children would plot at the lunch and
recess periods as to how they could get her on that desk.
She was inadvertently offering them a reward for their un-
ruliness. Their attitude was much like that of Brer Rabbit
who begged the fox not to throw him in the briar patch.
There was nothing they wanted more.

One should never underestimate a child's awareness that
he is breaking the rules. I think most children are rather
analytical about their defiance of adult authority; they consider the deed in advance, weighing its probable consequences. If the odds are too great that justice will triumph,
they'll take a safer course. This characteristic is verified
in millions of homes where the youngster will push one parent to the limits of his tolerance, but will be a sweet angel
with the other. Mom whimpers, "Rick minds his dad per-
fectly, but he won't pay any attention to me." Good old
Rick has observed that mom is safer than dad.

To summarize this point, the parent must recognize that
the most successful techniques of control are those which
manipulate something important to the child. Minor pain
is one of those important variables. Words following words
carry little or no motivational power for the child. "Why
don't you do right, Jack? You don't hardly ever do right.
What am I going to do with you, son? Mercy me, it seems
like I'm always having to get on you. I just can't see why
you won't do what you're told. If one time, just one time,
you would act your age, etc." Jack endures these endless
tirades, month in, month out, year after year. Fortunately
for him, nature has equipped Jack with a mechanism that
allows him to turn it off. A man who lives by a railroad

track somehow fails to hear the trains going by; likewise, Jack finds it useful to ignore the unmeaningful noise in his environment. Jack (and all his contemporaries) would be much more willing to "do right" if it were clearly to his personal advantage to cooperate.

4. Don't saturate the child with excessive materialism

Despite the hardships of the Great Depression, at least one question was then easier to answer than it is today; how can I say "no" to my child's materialistic desires? It was very simple for parents to tell their children that they couldn't afford to buy them everything they wanted; dad could barely keep bread on the table. But in the opulent times, the parental task becomes more difficult. It takes considerably more courage to say, "No, I *won't* buy you Baby-Blow-Her-Nose," than it did to say, "I'm sorry, but you know we can't afford to buy that doll." The child's lust for expensive toys is carefully generated through millions of dollars spent on TV advertising by toy manufacturers. The commercials are skillfully made so that the toys look like full-sized copies of their real counterparts: jet airplanes, robot monsters, and automatic rifles. The little buyer sits open-mouthed in utter fascination. Five minutes later he begins a campaign that will eventually cost his dad $14.95 plus batteries and tax. The trouble is, Dad *can* afford to buy the new item, if not with cash, at least with his magic credit card. And when three other children on the block get the coveted toys, Mom and Dad begin to feel the pressure, and even the guilt. They feel selfish because they have indulged themselves for similar luxuries. Suppose the parents are courageous enough to resist the child's urging; the child is not blocked — grandparents are notoriously easy to "con." Even if the child is unsuccessful in getting his parents or grandpar-

ents to buy what he wants, there is an annual, foolproof resource: Santa Claus! When junior asks Santa to bring him
something, his parents are in an inescapable trap. What can
they say, "Santa can't afford it? !" Is Santa going to forget
and disappoint him? No, the toy will be on Santa's sleigh.

Some would ask, "And why not? Why shouldn't we let
our children enjoy the fruits of our good times?" Certainly I
would not deny the child a reasonable quantity of the things
he craves. But many American children are inundated with
excesses that work toward their detriment. It has been said
that prosperity offers a greater test of character than does
adversity, and I'm inclined to agree. There are few conditions that inhibit a sense of appreciation more than for a
child to feel he is entitled to whatever he wants, whenever
he wants it. It is enlightening to watch as a child tears
open stacks of presents at his birthday party or perhaps at
Christmas time. One after another, the expensive contents
are tossed aside with little more than a glance. The child's
mother is made uneasy by this lack of enthusiasm and appreciation, so she says, "Oh, Marvin! Look what it is! It's a
a little tape recorder! What do you say to Grandmother?
Give Grandmother a big hug. Did you hear me, Marvin? Go
give Grams a big hug and kiss." Marvin may or may not
choose to make the proper noises to Grandmother. His
lack of exuberance results from the fact that prizes which
are won cheaply are of little value, regardless of the cost to
the original purchaser.

There is another reason that the child should be denied
some of the things he thinks he wants. Although it sounds
paradoxical, you actually cheat him of pleasure when you
give him too much. A classic example of this saturation
principle is evident in my household each year during the
Thanksgiving season. Our family is blessed with several of
the greatest cooks who ever ruled a kitchen, and once a

year they do their "thing." The traditional Thanksgiving dinner consists of turkey, dressing, cranberries, mashed potatoes, sweet potatoes, peas, hot rolls, two kinds of salads, and six or eight other dishes. Our behavior at this table is disgraceful, but wonderful. Everyone eats until he is uncomfortable, not saving room for dessert. Then the apple pie, pound cake, and fresh ambrosia are brought to the table. It just doesn't seem possible that we could eat another bite, yet somehow we do. Finally, taut family members begin to stagger away from their plates, looking for a place to fall. Later, about three o'clock in the afternoon, the internal pressure begins to subside, and someone passes the candy around. As the usual time for the evening meal arrives, no one is hungry, yet we've come to expect three meals a day. Turkey and roll sandwiches are constructed and consumed, followed by another helping of pie. By this time, everyone is a bit blunk-eyed, absent-mindedly eating what they neither want nor enjoy. This ridiculous ritual continues for two or three days, until the thought of food becomes rather disgusting. Whereas eating ordinarily offers one of life's greatest pleasures, it loses its thrill when the appetite for food is satiated.

Pleasure occurs when an intense need is satisfied. If there is no need, there is no pleasure. A glass of water is worth more than gold to a man dying of thirst. The analogy to children should be obvious. If you never allow a child to want something, he never enjoys the pleasure of receiving it. If you buy him a tricycle before he can walk, and a bicycle before he can ride, and a car before he can drive, and a diamond ring before he knows the value of money, he accepts these gifts with little pleasure and less appreciation. How unfortunate that such a child never had the chance to long for something, dreaming about it at night and plotting for it by day. He might have even gotten desperate enough

to work for it. The same possession that brought a yawn
could have been a trophy and a treasure. I suggest that you
allow your child the thrill of temporary deprivation; it's
more fun and *much* less expensive.

5. *Avoid extremes in control* and *love*

There is little question about the consequences of disciplinary extremes. On the side of harshness, a child suffers
the humiliation of total domination. The atmosphere is icy
and rigid, and he lives in constant fear. He is unable to
make his own decisions and his personality is squelched be-
neath the hobnailed boot of parental authority. Lasting
characteristics of dependency, overwhelming hostility, and
psychosis can emerge from this overbearing oppression. The
opposite position, ultimate permissiveness, is equally tragic.
Under this setting, the child is his own master from his
earliest babyhood. He thinks the world revolves around his
heady empire, and he often has utter contempt and disrespect for those closest to him. Anarchy and chaos reign in
his home, and his mother is often the most nervous, frustrated woman on her block. When the child is young, the
mother is stranded at home because she is too embarrassed
to take her little devil anywhere. It would be worth enduring the hardships if this confusion produced healthy, secure
children. Unfortunately the child usually suffers the most
difficulties from such anarchistic circumstances. This book
began by emphasizing the hazards and social consequences
of the extreme permissive approach to child rearing. But if
there is anything I don't want to do, it is to cause parents to
overreact, committing the opposite sin. Both extremes are
disastrous. There is safety only in the middle ground, which
is sometimes difficult to locate.

Extreme degrees of love can also be unhealthy for a child.

The complete absence of love (rejection) will destroy him emotionally, and in some cases physically. It has been known for several decades that an infant who is not loved, touched, and caressed will often die. Evidence of this fact was observed as early as the thirteenth century, when Frederick II conducted an experiment with fifty infants. He wanted to see what language the children would speak if they never had the opportunity to hear the spoken word. To accomplish this dubious research project, he assigned foster mothers to bathe and suckle the children, but forbade them to fondle, pet, or talk to their charges. The experiment failed because all fifty infants died. Hundreds of more recent studies indicate that the mother-child relationship during the first year of life is apparently vital to the infant's survival. An unloved child is truely the saddest phenomenon in all of nature.

While the absence of love has a predictable effect on children, it is not so well known that excessive love or "super love" has its hazards, too. Even some venerable experts, like Dr. Karl Menninger, do not acknowledge the dangers of excessive parental affection. Despite my respect for Dr. Menninger, I must disagree with his view that no child has ever been spoiled by love, and that a spoiled child is one who has been neglected by being ignored, or has been terrorized by threats of retribution for his mischief or has been bribed by indulgence. I believe some children *are* spoiled by love. Americans are tremendously child-oriented at this stage in their history; many parents have invested all of their hopes, dreams, desires, and ambitions in their youngsters. The natural culmination of this philosophy is overprotection of the next generation. I dealt with one anxious parent who stated that her children were the *only* sources of her satisfaction. During the long summers, she spent most of her time sitting at the front room window, watching her three girls while they played. She feared that they might get hurt or need her assistance; or they might ride their bikes in the street. Her responsibilities to her husband were sacrificed, despite his vigorous complaints. She did not have time to clean her house; guard duty at the window was her only function. She suffered enormous tensions over the known and unknown threats that could destroy her beloved offspring.

Childhood illness and sudden danger are always difficult for a loving parent to tolerate, but the slightest threat produces unbearable anxiety for the overprotective mom and dad. Unfortunately, the overprotective parent is not the only one who suffers; the child is often its victim, too. It has been theorized that asthma is more likely to occur in a "smother-loved" child, although the relationship has not been established conclusively. Other consequences of overprotection are less speculative. The overprotective parent finds it difficult to allow her child to take reasonable risks; those risks are a necessary prelude to maturity. Likewise, the materialistic problems described in the previous section are often maximized in a family where the children are so badly needed by one or both parents. Prolonged emotional immaturity is another frequent consequence of overprotection.

I have attempted to show how the extreme approaches to control and love are individually harmful. I should mention another unfortunate circumstance which occurs too often in our society. It is present in homes where the mother and father represent opposing extremes in control. The situation usually follows a familiar pattern: Dad is a very busy man, and he is deeply involved in his work. He is gone from early morning to night, and when he does return, he brings home a briefcase full of work. Perhaps he travels frequently. During the rare times when he is home and not working, he is exhausted. He collapses in front of the TV set to watch a ball game and he doesn't want to be bothered. Consequently, his approach to child control is rather harsh and unsympathetic. His temper flares regularly and the children learn to stay out of his way. By contrast, Mom has no outside world from which to derive personal satisfaction. Her home and her children are her sources of joy; in fact, they have replaced the romantic fires which have vanished from her marriage. She worries about Dad's lack of affection and tenderness for the children. She feels that she should compensate for his sternness by leaning in the other direction. When he sends the children to bed without their supper, she slips them some milk and cookies. Since she is the only authority on the scene when Dad is gone, the predominant tone in the home is one of unstructured permissiveness. She needs the children too much to risk trying to control them. Thus, the two parental symbols of authority act to contradict each other, and the child is caught somewhere between them. The child respects neither parent because each has assassinated the authority of the other. It has been my observation that these self-destructing forms of authority often load a time-bomb of rebellion that discharges during adolescence. The most hostile, aggressive teen-agers I have known have emerged from this antithetical combination.

The "middle ground" of love and control must be sought if we are to produce healthy, responsible children.

SUMMARY

Lest I be misunderstood, I shall emphasize my message by stating its opposite. I am not recommending that your home be harsh and oppressive. I am not suggesting that you give your children a spanking every morning with their ham and eggs, or that you make your boys sit in the living room with their hands folded and their legs crossed. (Children are like clocks; they must be allowed to run.) I am not proposing that you try to make adults out of your little children so you can impress your adult friends with your parental skill, or that you punish your children whimsically, swinging and screaming when they didn't know they were wrong. I am not suggesting that you insulate your dignity and authority by being cold and unapproachable. These parental tactics do not produce healthy, responsible children. By contrast, I am recommending a simple principle: when you are defiantly challenged, win decisively. When the child asks, "Who's in charge?" tell him. When he mutters, "Who loves me?" take him in your arms and surround him with affection. Treat him with respect and dignity, and expect the same from him. Then begin to enjoy the sweet benefits of competent parenthood.

QUESTIONS AND ANSWERS

Listed below are a few of the questions I have been asked in my casework with parents and by various groups to whom I have spoken. Many of these items were selected from actual tape recordings, representing the recurring themes for which answers were sought.

1. My son will obey me at home, but he becomes difficult to manage whenever I take him to a public place, like a restaurant. Then he embarrasses me in front of other people. Why is he like that? How can I change him?

Many parents do not like to punish or correct their children in public places where their discipline is observed by critical onlookers. They'll enforce good behavior at home, but the child is "safe" when unfamiliar adults are around. In this situation, it is easy to see what the child has observed. He has learned that public facilities are a sanctuary where he can act any way he wishes. His parents are in a corner because of their self-imposed restriction. The remedy for this situation is simple: when little Roger decides to disobey in public, take him by the arm and march him out of the presence of your observers. Then respond as you would at home. Roger will then learn that the same rules apply everywhere, and that the sanctuaries are not really so safe after all.

2. We hear so much about the importance of communication between a parent and child. If you suppress a child's defiant behavior, how can he express the hostility and resentment he feels?

The child should be free to say *anything* to his parent, including "I don't like you, Daddy," or "You weren't fair with me, Mother." These expressions of true feeling should not be suppressed, provided they are said in a respectful manner. There is a thin line between what is acceptable and unacceptable behavior at this point. The child's expression of strong feeling, even resentment and hostility, should be encouraged if it exists. But the parent should prohibit the child from resorting to name-calling and open rebellion. "Daddy, you hurt my feelings in front of my friends and you were unkind to me" is an acceptable statement; "You stupid idiot, why didn't you shut up when my friends were here? !" is obviously unacceptable. If approached rationally as depicted in the first statement, it would be wise for daddy to sit down and try to understand the child's viewpoint. Dad should be big enough to apologize to the child if he feels he was wrong. If he was right, however, he should calmly explain why he reacted as he did and tell the child how they can avoid the collision next time. It is possible to communicate without sacrificing parental respect, and the child should be taught how to express his discontent.

3. How long do you think a child should be allowed to cry after being punished or spanked? Is there a limit?

Yes, I believe there should be a limit. As long as the tears represent a genuine release of emotion, they should be permitted to fall. But crying quickly changes from inner sobbing to an exterior weapon. It becomes a tool of protest to punish the enemy. Real crying usually lasts two minutes or less, but may continue for five. After that point, the child is merely complaining, and the change can be recognized in the tone and intensity of his voice. I would require him to stop the protest crying, usually by offering him a little more of whatever caused the original tears. In less antagonistic moments the crying can easily be stopped by getting the child interested in something else.

4. Permissiveness is a relative term. Please describe its meaning to you.

When I use the term permissiveness, I refer to the absence of effective parental authority, resulting in the lack of boundaries for the child. This word represents childish disrespect, defiance, and the general confusion that occurs in the absence of adult leadership.

5. We have an adopted child who came to us when he was two years old. He was so abused during those first couple of years that my husband and I cannot let ourselves punish him, even when he deserves it. We also feel we don't have the right to discipline him, since we are not his real parents. Are we doing right?

I'm afraid you are making a mistake commonly committed by the parents of adopted children. They pity their youngsters too much to control them. They feel that life has already been too harsh with the little ones, and they must not make things worse by disciplining them. As you indicated, there is often the feeling that they do not have the right to make demands on their adopted children. These guilt-laden attitudes can lead to unfortunate consequences. Transplanted children have the same needs for guidance and discipline as those remaining with their natural parents. One of the surest ways to make a child feel insecure is to treat him as though he is different — unusual — brittle. If the parents view him as an unfortunate waif to be shielded, he will see himself that way too.

Parents of sick and deformed children are also likely to find discipline harder to implement. A child with a withered arm or some nonfatal illness can become a little terror, simply because the usual behavioral boundaries are not established by his parents. It must be remembered that the need to be controlled and governed is almost universal in childhood; this need is not eliminated by other problems and difficulties in life. In some cases, the desire for boundaries is maximized by other troubles, for it is through loving control that parents express personal worth to a child.

6. Do you think a child should be required to say "thank you" and "please" around the house?

I sure do. Requiring these phrases is one method of reminding the child that this is not a "gimmie-gimmie" world. Even though his mother is cooking for him and buying for him and giving to him, he must assume a few attitudinal responsibilities in return. As I said before, appreciation must be taught and this instructional process begins with fundamental politeness.

7. How do you feel about working mothers?

Motherhood is a full-time job during the child's first five years. I know some families which just can't seem to pay their bills without a supplement to the father's paycheck, but children need their mother more than they do a newer car or larger house. The issue is not so much, "Should mom work?" as it is "Who will take her place?" Is an eighteen-year-old baby sitter going to apply the principles of good parenthood which I've outlined? Is she going to mold and guide and reinforce those subtle but important attitudes that emerge each day? Is she capable of disciplining and loving in the proper combination? Being a good mother is one of the most complex skills in life, yet this role has fallen into disrepute in recent years. What activity could be more important than shaping human lives during their impressionable and plastic years? I'm afraid I have little patience with the view that domestic responsibilities are not worthy of a woman's time. The hand that rocks the cradle rules the world, yet mom is now told that she should chase around after some additional source of fulfillment. The cigarette commercial tells her, "You've come a long way, baby," but that image portrayed makes me want to say, "Yes, but you've still got a long way to go, baby." The traditional concept of motherhood, *full-time* motherhood, still sounds like a pretty good idea to me.

8. I have never spanked my three-year-old because I am afraid it will teach her to hit others and be a violent person. Do you think I am wrong?

I believe you are, but you've made an important point. It *is* possible for parents to create hostility and aggressiveness in their children by behaving violently themselves. If they scream and yell, lashing out emotionally and flailing the children for their accidents and mistakes, they serve as models for their children to imitate. That kind of parental violence is worlds apart from the proper disciplinary approach. However, when the child has lowered his head and clenched his fist, he is daring the parent to take him on. If the parent responds appropriately (on the backside) he has taught the child a valuable lesson that is consistent with nature's method of instruction. Consider the purpose of pain in life. Suppose two-year-old Peter is pulling on the tablecloth and with it comes a vase of roses which tips over the edge of the table, cracking him between the eyes. Peter is in great pain. From this pain he learns that it is dangerous to pull on the tablecloth. Likewise, he presses his arm against a hot stove and quickly learns that fire must be treated with respect. He pulls the doggie's tail and promptly receives a neat row of teeth marks across the back of his hand. He climbs over the side of his high chair when mom isn't looking and he learns all about gravity. For three or four years, he accumulates bumps and bruises and scratches and burns, each one teaching him about life's boundaries. Do these experiences make him a violent person? No! The pain associated with these events teaches him to avoid making those same mistakes again. God created this mechanism as the child's best vehicle for instruction. The loving parent can and should make use of the same processes in teaching him about certain kinds of social dangers. Contrary to what it might seem, Peter is more likely to be a violent person if his parent fails to apply this principle, because he learns too late about the painful consequences of acting selfishly, rebelliously, and aggressively.

9. You mentioned boundaries a moment ago. Does a child really want to have limits set on his behavior?

Most certainly! After working with children for these

years, I could not be more convinced of this fact. They derive security from knowing where the boundaries are. Perhaps an illustration will make this more clear. Imagine yourself driving a car over the Royal Gorge in Colorado. The bridge is suspended hundreds of feet above the canyon floor, and as a first-time traveler, you are tense as you drive across. (I knew one little fellow who was so awed by the view over the side of the bridge that he said, "Wow, Daddy. If you fell off of here it'd kill you constantly!") Now suppose that there were no guardrails on the side of the bridge; where would you steer the car? Right down the middle of the road! Even though you don't plan to hit those protective rails along the side, you feel more secure just knowing they are there. The analogy to children has been demonstrated empirically. During the early days of the progressive education movement, one enthusiastic theorist decided to take down the chain-link fence that surrounded the nursery school yard. He thought the children would feel more freedom of movement without that visible barrier surrounding them. When the fence was removed, however, the boys and girls huddled near the center of the play yard. Not only did they not wander away, they didn't even venture to the edge of the grounds.

There is security in defined limits. When the home atmosphere is as it should be, the child lives in utter safety. He never gets in trouble unless he deliberately asks for it, and as long as he stays within the limits, there is mirth and freedom and acceptance. If this is what is meant by "democracy" in the home, then I favor it. If it means the absence of boundaries, or that each child sets his own boundaries, then I'm inalterably opposed to it.

10. Should a child be punished for wetting the bed? How can you deal with this difficult problem?

Unless it occurs after the child is awake, bed-wetting (enuresis) is an involuntary act for which he is not responsible. Punishment under those circumstances is unforgiveable and disastrous. He is humiliated by the incident, anyway, and the more frequently it happens, the more foolish he feels about it. The bed-wetter needs considerable reassurance and patience from his mom, and she should try to conceal his problem from those who would laugh at him. Even good-natured humor within the family is painful when it is at his expense.

Bed-wetting has been the subject of much research, and there are several different causes in individual cases. In some children, the problem is physiological, resulting from a small bladder or other physical difficulty. A urologist may be consulted in the diagnosis and treatment of such cases. For others, the problem is unquestionably emotional in origin. Any change in the psychological environment of the home may produce midnight moisture. During summer camps conducted for young children, the directors often put rubber sheets on the beds of all the little visitors. The anxiety associated with being away from home apparently causes a high probability of bed-wetting during the first few nights, and it is particularly risky to be sleeping on one of the lower levels of the stacked bunk beds. There is a third factor that I feel is the most frequent cause of enuresis. During the child's toddler years, he wets the bed because he simply has not mastered nighttime bladder control. His mother habitually gets him up at night, taking him to the potty. There he is, sound asleep, being told to "go tinkle" or whatever. Thus, as he grows older, the practice continues. When he needs to urinate at night, he dreams he is being told to turn loose; anytime he is partially awakened or disturbed at night, he believes he is being ushered to the bathroom. I would recommend that the parents of older bed-wetters stop getting them up at night, even if the bed-wetting continued for a while. There are other mechanical remedies which work in some cases, such as electronic devices that ring a bell and awaken the child when the urine completes an electrical circuit. A pediatrician or child psychologist can guide you in seeking a solution to this inconvenient problem. In the meantime, it is important to help the child maintain his self-respect despite his embarrassing flaw, and by all means, conceal your displeasure if it exists.

11. I have spanked my children for their disobedience and it didn't seem to help. Does this approach fail with some children?

Children are so tremendously variable that it is sometimes hard to believe that they are all members of the same human family. You can crush some children with nothing more than a stern look; others seem to require strong and even painful disciplinary measures to make a vivid impression. This difference usually results from the degree to which a child needs adult approval and acceptance. As I said earlier, the primary parental task is to get behind the eyes of the child, thereby tailoring the discipline to his unique perception.

In a direct answer to the question, it is not this individual variation that causes spanking to be ineffectual in most cases. When disciplinary measures fail, it is usually because of fundamental errors in their application. It is possible for twice the amount of punishment to yield half the results. I have made a study of situations where the parent has told me that the child ignores the spankings he receives, going back to violate the same rule. There are four basic reasons for the lack of success: (1) The most recurring problem results from infrequent, whimsical punishment. Half the time the child is not punished for a particular act of defiance; the other half of the time he is cuffed about for it. Children need to know the certainty of justice. (2) The child may be more strong-willed than the parent, and they both know it. If he can outlast a temporary onslaught, he has won a major battle, eliminating punishment as a tool in the parents repertoire. Even though Mom spanks him, he wins the battle by defying her again. The solution to this situation is obvious: outlast him; win, even if it takes a repeated measure. The experience will be painful for both participants, but the benefits will come tomorrow and tomorrow and tomorrow. (3) The parent suddenly decides to employ this form of punishment after doing nothing for a year or two prior to that time. It takes a child a while to respond to a new procedure in this manner, and the parent might get discouraged during the adjustment period. (4) The spanking may be too gentle. If it doesn't hurt, it isn't worth avoiding next time. A slap with the hand on the bottom of a multi-diapered thirty-month old is not a deterrent to anything. It isn't necessary to beat a child, but he should be able to feel the message.

12. We hear a lot about the "battered child" syndrome today. What kind of parent would beat up a defenseless little child? How serious is the problem?

The problem of the battered child is much greater than is generally realized. Dr. James Apthorp, assistant professor of pediatrics at the University of Southern California School of Medicine, stated recently that more children under five years of age are killed by their own parents than die of disease. He estimated that 60,000 children are beaten to death annually in America. The beatings are rarely premeditated; they may occur when an ordinary spanking gets out of hand, or when an emotionally disturbed parent loses control. Child abuse is committed by parents in all races and socio-economic levels, although younger parents of lower intelligence are the most likely to become violent with their children.

It is certainly pitiful to see the broken, bruised, and starved children who are brought in depressing numbers to hospitals for children. The little victims are too young to defend themselves or even call for help, and some of the atrocities are terribly pathetic. Several years ago, for example, one emotionally disturbed mother destroyed her infant daughter's eyes with a razor blade. Another four-year-old girl was abandoned on a freeway late one night, where she clung to the center divider for eleven hours before being rescued by the police. Such abused children often grow up to become brutal parents themselves, inflicting similar pain on their own children.

One of my greatest concerns in recommending corporal punishment (spanking) is that some parents might apply the thrashings too frequently or too severely. Generally, however, parents are less likely to become violent with their children when they know how to handle small behavioral problems before they reach a stage of extreme irritation.

13. If it is natural for a toddler to break all the rules, should he be punished for his defiance?

Many of the spankings and slaps given to toddlers could and should be avoided. They get in trouble most frequently because of their natural desire to touch, bite, taste, smell, and break everything within their grasp. However, this "reaching out" behavior is not aggressive. It is a valuable technique for learning and should not be discouraged. I have seen parents slap their two-year-old throughout the day for simply investigating his world. This squelching of normal curiosity is not fair to the youngster. It seems foolish to leave an expensive trinket where it will tempt him, and then lash him for taking the bait. If little fat-fingers insists on handling the china cups on the lower shelf, it is much wiser to distract him with something else than to pound him for his persistence. Toddlers cannot resist the offer of a new plaything; they are amazingly easy to interest in less fragile toys, and mother should keep a few alternate goodies available for use when needed.

When, then, should the toddler be subjected to mild punishment? When he openly defies his parents' spoken commands! If he runs the other way when called — if he slams his milk on the floor — if he screams and throws a tantrum at bedtime — if he hits his friends — these are the forms of unacceptable behavior which should be discouraged. Even in these situations, however, all-out spankings are not often required to eliminate the response. A firm thump on the head or a rap on the fingers will convey the same message just as convincingly. Spankings should be reserved for his moments of greatest antagonism.

I feel it is important to stress the point made earlier: the toddler years are critical to the child's future attitude toward authority. He should be patiently taught to obey without being expected to behave like an adult.

14. Should teen-age children be spanked for disobedience or rudeness?

No! Teen-agers desperately want to be thought of as adults, and they deeply resent being treated like children. Spanking is the ultimate insult. Punishment for adolescents should involve lost privileges, financial deprivation, and related forms of non-physical retribution.

15. Sometimes my husband and I disagree on our discipline, and we will argue about what is best in front of the child. Do you think this is damaging?

Yes, I do. You and your husband should agree to go along with the decision of the other, at least in front of the child. The wisdom of the matter can be discussed later. When the two of you contradict each other, right and wrong begin to appear arbitrary to the child.

16. My husband and I are divorced, so I have to handle all the discipline of the children myself. How does this change the recommendations you've made?

Not at all. The principles of good discipline remain the same, regardless of the family setting. The procedures do become somewhat harder for one parent, like yourself, to implement, since you have no one to support you when the children become defiant. You have to play the role of father *and* mother, which is not easily done. Nevertheless, children do not make allowances for your handicap. You must demand their respect or you will not receive it.

17. Do you think parents are now beginning to value discipline more? Is the day of permissiveness over?

Parents who tried extreme permissiveness have seen its failure, for the most part. Unfortunately, those parents will soon be grandparents, and the world will profit little from their experience. What worries me most is the kind of discipline that will be exercised by the generation now reaching young adulthood. Many of these new parents have never seen good discipline exercised. They have had no model. Besides this, they have severed themselves from their best source of information, avowing that anyone over thirty is to be mistrusted. It will be interesting to see what develops from this blind date between mom and baby.

II

The Miracle Tools

In the preceding chapter, we dealt with the proper parental response to a child's defiant "challenging behavior." Now we turn our attention to the leadership of children where antagonism is not involved. There are countless situations where the parent wishes to increase the child's level of responsibility, but that task is not easy. How can a mother get her child to brush his teeth regularly, or pick up his clothes, or display table manners? How can she teach him to be more responsible with money? What can the parent do to eliminate obnoxious habits, such as whining, sloppiness, or apparent laziness? Is there a solution to perpetual tardiness? These kinds of behavior do not involve direct confrontations between parent and child, and should not be handled in the same forceful manner described previously. It would be unwise and unfair to punish a youngster for his understandable immaturity and childishness. A much more effective technique is available for use by the knowledgeable parent.

The most magnificent theory ever devised for the control of behavior is called the "Law of Reinforcement," formulated

many years ago by the first educational psychologist, E. L.
Thorndike. It is magnificent because it works! Thorndike's
original law has been honed to a sharp edge of effectiveness
by the work of B. F. Skinner, who described the conditions
under which the principles work most effectively. Stated
simply, the Law of Reinforcement reads, "Behavior which
achieves desirable consequences will recur." In other words,
if an individual likes what happens as a result of his behavior, he will be inclined to repeat that act. If Sally gets
favorable attention from the boys on the day she wears a
new dress, she will want to wear the dress again and again.
If Pancho wins with one tennis racket and loses with another,
he will prefer the racket with which he has found success.
This principle is disarmingly simple, but it has profound
implications for human learning.

I utilized these techniques in teaching my little dachs-
hund, Sigmund Freud (Siggy), to sit up. Now most dachs-
hunds will sit up without being taught to do so, because it
is a natural response for the long-bodied animals to make.
But not Siggy! He is unquestionably the world's most independent animal. During the first year of his life, I thought
he was a little bit "slow" between the ears; the second year
I began to think he might be mentally retarded; now, however, I see him as a recalcitrant, stubborn rascal who just
wants to do things his own way. It is difficult to entice Siggy
to cooperate in any self-improvement program without offering him an edible incentive. He is particularly fond of
cookies, and I utilized this interest to good advantage. I
propped him in a vertical position where he remained for
only a second or two before falling. Then I gave him an
old-fashioned, chocolate chip cookie. He loved it. I sat
him up again, and I fed him the goodie as he was falling.
Siggy bounced all around the room, trying to take the remaining cookies away from me — but there was only one

way to continue the snack. Even Siggy began to see that reality. In less than thirty minutes of this ridiculous exercise, he received the message loud and clear. He has not had all four feet on the ground since that time! Throughout the day, he can be found propped on his haunches, asking for a bite of something — anything. Now I'm almost sorry I started the game because I feel guilty in ignoring him. After all, it was my idea in the first place; I am compelled to find him something to eat in the kitchen.

This reinforcement technique was useful in teaching Siggy to go chase a ball (a fantastic demonstration of animal intelligence). I threw the ball about ten feet out in front of us, then dragged Sig by the nape of the neck to where it lay. I opened his mouth, put the ball in place, and dragged him back to the starting place. An oatmeal cookie was waiting at the finish line. It was even easier to get his cooperation this time because he began to grasp the concept of working for a reward. That idea is now firmly ingrained and he has become rather creative in applying it to his advantage. If the family happens to eat dinner from trays in order to watch the evening television news, Siggy stations himself in the exact spot where everyone's line of vision crosses on the way to the tube. There he sits, weaving back and forth perpetually.

More serious attempts have been made to teach sophisticated behavior to animals by the principles of reinforcement, and the results have been remarkable. A pigeon has been taught to examine radio tubes moving by on a conveyor belt. The bird will evaluate each tube and knock the defective ones off the track, for which he receives a pellet of grain. He will sit there all day long, concentrating on his work. As one might imagine, the labor unions take a dim view of this process; the pigeon does not demand coffee breaks or other fringe benefits, and his wages are disgracefully low. Other animals have been made to perform virtually human feats by the careful application of rewards.

Rewards are not only useful in shaping animal behavior; they succeed even better with humans. However, it is not sufficient to dole out gifts and prizes in an unplanned manner. There are specific principles which must be followed if the Law of Reinforcement is to achieve its full potential. Let's consider the elements of this technique in detailed application to children.

1. Rewards must be granted immediately

If the maximum effectiveness is to be obtained from a reward, it should be offered shortly after the desirable behavior has occurred. Parents often make the mistake of offering long-range rewards to children, but their successes are few. It is usually unfruitful to offer nine-year-old Joey a car when he is sixteen if he'll work hard in school during the next seven years. Second and third grade elementary children are often promised a trip to grandma's house next summer in exchange for good behavior throughout the year. Their obedience is typically unaffected by this lure. It is unsatisfactory to offer Mary Lou a new doll for Christmas if she'll keep her room straight in July. Most children have neither the mental capacity nor the maturity to hold a long-range goal in mind day after day. Time moves slowly for them; consequently, the reinforcement seems impossible to reach and uninteresting to contemplate. For animals, a reward should be offered approximately two seconds after the behavior has occurred. A mouse will learn the turns in a maze much faster if the cheese is waiting at the end than he will when a five-second delay is imposed. Although children can tolerate longer delays than animals, the power of a reward is weakened with time.

Immediate reinforcement has been utilized successfully in the treatment of childhood autism, a major disorder which resembles childhood schizophrenia. The autistic child does not relate to his parents or any other people; he has no language; he usually displays bizarre, uncontrollable behavior. There are those professionals who believe autism results from early difficulties in the relationship between a child and his mother; I cannot accept that hypothesis. The evidence seems to point toward the existence of a biochemical malfunction in the autistic child's neural apparatus. For whatever cause, autism is extremely resistant to treatment. How can a therapist help a child who can neither talk nor relate to him? All prior forms of treatment have been discouragingly ineffective, which led researchers to experiment with the use of rewards. At the University of California at Los Angeles, autistic children are now placed on a program designed to encourage speech. At first, a bit of chocolate candy is tossed into the child's mouth whenever he utters a sound of any kind; his grunts, groans, and growls are rewarded similarly. The next step is to reward the child for more specific vowel sounds. When an "o" sound is to be taught, candy is paid for all accidental noises in the proper direction. As the child progresses, he is finally required to pronounce the names of certain objects or people to achieve the reinforcement. Two-word phrases are then sought, followed by more complicated sentence structure. Considerable language has been taught to these difficult children by this simple procedure. The same technique has been employed simultaneously in teaching the autistic child to respond to the people around him. He is placed in a small, dark box which has one sliding wooden window. The therapist sits on the outside of the box, facing the child who peers out the window. As long as the child looks at the therapist, the window remains open. However, when his mind wanders and he begins to gaze around, the panel falls, leaving him in the dark for a few seconds. Although I know of no child with severe autism who has been successfully transformed into a normal individual, the use of reinforcement therapy has brought some of these patients to a state of conversant, civilized behavior. The key to this success has been the immediate application of a pleasant consequence to desired behavior.

Immediate reinforcement is the most useful technique available to parents in teaching responsibility to their children. Parents often complain about the irresponsibility of their youngsters, yet they fail to realize that this lack of industriousness has been *learned*. *All* human behavior is learned — the desirable and the undesirable responses. Children learn to laugh, play, run, and jump; they also learn to whine, bully, pout, fight, throw temper tantrums, or be tomboys. The universal teacher is reinforcement. The child repeats the behavior which he considers to be successful. A youngster may be cooperative and helpful because he enjoys the effect that behavior has on his parents; another will sulk and pout for the same reason. When parents recognize characteristics which they dislike in their children, they should set about *teaching* more admirable traits by allowing good behavior to succeed and bad behavior to fail.

Described below are the steps of a program devised by Dr. Malcolm Williamson and myself for use with children between four and six years of age; it can be modified in accordance with the age and maturity of the youngster.

1. The chart on the next page lists some responsibilities and behaviors which the parent may wish to instill. These fourteen items constitute a much greater degree of cooperation and effort than most five-year-old children display on a daily basis, but the proper use of rewards can make it seem more like fun than work. *Immediate*

"My Jobs"

	November	14	15	16	17	18	19	20	21	22	23	24	25	26	27	28	29	30
1. I brushed my teeth without being told																		
2. I straightened my room before bedtime																		
3. I picked up my clothes without being told																		
4. I fed the fish without being told																		
5. I emptied the trash without being told																		
6. I minded Mommie today																		
7. I minded Daddy today																		
8. I said my prayers tonight																		
9. I was kind to little brother Billy today																		
10. I took my vitamin pill																		
11. I said "thank you" and "please" today																		
12. I went to bed last night without complaining																		
13. I gave clean water to the dog today																		
14. I washed my hands and came to the table when called																		
TOTAL:																		

reinforcement is the key: each evening, colored dots (preferably red) or stars should be placed by the behaviors that were done satisfactorily. If dots are not available, the squares can be colored with a felt-tip pen; however, the child should be allowed to chalk up his own successes.

2. A penny should be granted for every behavior done properly in a given day; if more than three items are missed in one day, *no* pennies should be given.

3. Since a child can earn a maximum of fourteen cents a day, the parent has an excellent opportunity to teach him how to manage his money. It is suggested that he be allowed to spend only ten to twenty cents per week of these earnings. Special trips to the candy store or toy shop can be planned. The daily ice cream truck provides a handy source of reinforcement. Of the remaining eighty-eight cents (maximum) the child can be required to give ten cents in the church offering or to some other charitable recipient; he should then save about thirty-five cents per week. The final twenty or thirty cents can be accumulated for a long-range expenditure for something he wants or needs.

4. The list of behaviors to be rewarded does *not* remain static. Once the child has got into the habit of hanging up his clothes, or feeding the puppy, or brushing his teeth, the parent should then substitute new responsibilities. A new chart should be made each month, and Junior can make suggestions for his revised chart.

This system provides several side benefits, in addition to the main objective of teaching responsible behavior. Through its use, for example, the child learns to count. He is taught to give to worthy causes. He begins to understand the concept of saving. He learns to restrict and control his emotional impulses. And finally, he is taught the meaning of money and how to spend it wisely. The advantages to his parents are equally impressive. A father of four young children applied the technique and later told me that the noise level in his household had been reduced noticeably.

If this kind of reinforcement is so successful, why has it not been used more widely? The answer to this question is an unfortunate one: adults are reluctant to utilize rewards because they view them as a source of bribery. Our most workable teaching device is ignored because of a philosophical misunderstanding. Our entire society is established on a system of reinforcement, yet we don't want to apply it where it is needed most: with young children. As adults, we go to work each day and receive a paycheck on Friday. Getting out of bed each morning is rewarded regularly. Medals are given to brave soldiers; plaques are awarded to successful businessmen; watches are presented to retiring employees. Rewards make responsible effort worthwhile. The main reason for the overwhelming success of capitalism is that hard work and personal discipline are rewarded materially. The great weakness of socialism is the absence of reinforcement; why should a man struggle to achieve if there is nothing special to be gained? The most distasteful aspect of my brief military experience was the absence of reinforcement; I could not get a higher rank until a certain period of time had passed, no matter how hard I worked. The size of my pay check was determined by Congress, not by my competence or output. This system is a destroyer of motivation, yet some parents seem to feel it is the only appropriate one for children. They expect little Marvin to carry responsibility simply because it is noble for him to do so. They want him to work and learn and sweat for the sheer joy of personal discipline. He isn't going to buy it!

Consider the alternative approach to the "bribery" I've recommended. How are *you* going to get your five-year-old to perform the behaviors listed on the chart? The most frequently used substitutes are nagging, complaining, begging,

screaming, threatening, and punishing. The mother who
objects to the use of rewards may also go to bed each evening with a headache, vowing to have no more children.
She didn't like to accentuate materialism in this manner,
yet later she will give money to her child. Since her youngster never handles his own cash, he doesn't learn how to save
it or spend it wisely. The toys she buys him are purchased
with her money, and he values them less. But most important, he is not learning self-discipline and personal responsibility that is possible through the careful reinforcement of
that behavior.

I watched the application of these contrasting viewpoints
in two actual home situations: Daren's parents felt that he
had certain responsibilities as a member of the family. Consequently, he was not rewarded (paid) for his efforts around
the home. Daren hated his work because there was no personal gain involved in the effort; it was something to be tol-
erated. When he had to clean out the garage on Saturday, he
would drag himself out to the disaster area and gaze with
unfocused eyes at the depressing task before him. As might
be expected, he did a miserably poor job because he was
absolutely devoid of motivation. This sloppiness brought a
tongue-lashing from his dad, which hardly made the experience a pleasant one. Daren's parents were not stingy with
him. They supplied his needs and even gave him some
spending money; when the State Fair came to town, they
would give him $5.00 to spend. Because their gifts were
not linked to his responsible efforts, the money provided no
source of motivation. Daren grew up hating to work; his
parents had inadvertently reinforced his irresponsibility.

Brian's parents took a different view. They felt that he
should be paid for the tasks that went beyond his regular
household duties. He was not rewarded for carrying out the
trash or straightening his room, but he received money for

working in the yard on Saturday. This hourly wage was a respectable amount, comparable to what he could earn outside the family. Brian loved his work. He'd get up in the morning and attack the weeds in his backyard; he would count his money and work and look at his watch and work and count his money. At times he rushed home from school to get in an hour or two before dark. He opened his own bank account, and was very careful about how he surrendered his hard-earned cash. Brian enjoyed great status in his neighborhood because he always had money in his pocket. He didn't spend it very often, but he *could have done so* at any given moment. That was impressive power! At one point he drew all of his money out of the bank and asked for the total amount in new one dollar bills. He then stacked his twenty-eight bills in his top dresser drawer, and displayed them casually to Daren and his other penniless friends. Work and responsibility were the keys to this status, and he learned a good measure of both. His parents were careful never to give him a cent. They bought his clothes and necessities, but he purchased his own toys and personal indulgences. From an economic point of view, Brian's parents spent no more money than did Daren's mom and dad; they merely linked each penny to the behavior they desired. I believe their approach was the more productive of the two.

As implied before, it is very important to know when to use rewards and when to resort to punishment. It is not recommended that rewards be utilized when the child has challenged the authority of the parent. For example, mom may say, "Come here, Lucy," and Lucy shouts "No!" It is a mistake for mom to then offer a piece of candy if Lucy will comply with her request. She would actually be rewarding her for defiance. If there is still confusion about how to respond in this kind of direct conflict, I suggest the reader take another look at Chapter One of this book. Rewards should not be used as a substitute for authority; reward and punishment each has its place in child management, and reversals bring unfortunate results.

2. Rewards need not be material in nature

When my daughter was three years of age, I began to teach her some pre-reading skills, including the alphabet. By planning the training sessions to occur after dinner each evening, her dessert (bits of chocolate candy) provided the chief source of motivation. Late one afternoon I was sitting on the floor drilling her on several new letters when a tremendous crash shook the neighborhood. The whole family rushed outside immediately to see what had happened, and observed that a teen-ager had wrecked his car on our quiet residential street. The boy was not badly hurt, but his automobile was a mess. We sprayed the smoldering car with water to keep the dripping gas from igniting, and made the necessary phone call to the police. It was not until the excitement began to lessen that we realized our daughter had not followed us out of the house. I returned to the den where I found her elbow deep in the two-pound bag of candy I had left behind. She had put at least a pound of chocolate into her mouth, and most of the remainder was distributed around her chin, nose, and forehead. When she saw me coming, she managed to jam another handful into her chipmunk cheeks. From this experience, I learned one of the limitations of using material, or at least edible, reinforcement.

Anything that is considered desirable to an individual can serve as reinforcement for his behavior. The most obvious rewards for animals are those which satisfy physical needs, although humans are further motivated to resolve their overwhelming psychological needs. Some children, for example, would rather receive a sincere word of praise than a ten dollar bill, particularly if the adult approval is expressed in front of other children. Children and adults of all ages seek constant satisfaction of their emotional needs, including the desire for love, social acceptance, and self-respect. Additionally, they hope to find excitement, intellectual stimulation, entertainment, and pleasure.

Most children and adults seek to satisfy their psychological needs from contact with other people. Since we depend on our associates to convince us that we are loved, accepted, and respected, we are keenly interested in what those associates think and say. *As a result, verbal reinforcement can be the strongest motivator of human behavior.* Consider the tremendous impact of the following comments:

"Here comes Phil — the ugliest guy in school."

"Louise is so stupid! She never knows the right answer in class."

"Joe will strike out. He always does."

These unkind assessments burn like acid to the children they describe, causing them to modify future behavior. Phil may become quiet, withdrawn, and easily embarrassed. Louise will probably display even less interest in her schoolwork than before, appearing lazy to her teachers. Joe may give up baseball and other athletic endeavors.

We adults are equally sensitive to the idle comments of our peers. It is often humorous to observe how vulnerable we are to the casual remarks of our friends (and even our enemies). "You've gained a few pounds, haven't you, Martha?" Martha may choose to ignore the comment for the moment, but she will spend fifteen minutes before the mirror that evening and start an extensive diet program the next morning.

"Ralph is about your age, Pete; I'd say he is 46 or 48

years old." Pete is only 39, and the blood drains from his face; the new concern over his appearance may be instrumental in his decision to purchase a toupee the following month.

Our hearing apparatus is more attuned to this kind of personal evaluation than any other subject, and our sense of self-respect and worthiness emerge largely from these unintentional messages.

Despite our dependence on social feedback, we are surprisingly unaware of the degree to which we influence those around us. The next time the reader is involved in a three-way discussion, I suggest that he pause to observe the other participant who is not talking at the moment. With few exceptions, that listener will not be standing immobile and passive. He will probably be providing the talker with a steady stream of information, revealing how the spoken ideas are being received. As the talker rambles on, the listener is nodding his head, smiling in agreement, mumbling "Uh-huh" and "Yes, that's true." Or he may be expressing disagreement in a similar gesturing fashion. The talker is anything but immune to this evaluation of his thoughts; he sees the cues and alters his conversation accordingly. Enthusiastic responses from the listener will produce more excitement in the talker. If he is speaking on a controversial topic or a subject with which he is uneasy, he may "fish" for additional reinforcement, saying. "Haven't you found that true, Jack?" The listener then becomes the talker, and the feedback is provided to him in reverse. Social behavior is highly dependent on this kind of verbal reinforcement, occurring in everyday conversation. The same is true in the relationship between the parent and child, and the astute parent will capitalize on this pleasant source of motivation.

Verbal reinforcement should permeate the entire parent-child relationship. Too often our parental instruction consists of a million "don'ts" which are jammed down the child's throat. We should spend more time rewarding him for the behavior we do admire, even if our "reward" is nothing more than a sincere compliment. Remembering the child's need for self-esteem and acceptance, the wise parent can satisfy those important longings while using them to teach valued concepts and behavior. A few examples may be helpful:

> Mother to daughter: You certainly colored nicely within the lines on that picture, Rene. I like to see that kind of neat art work. I'm going to put this on the bulletin board in the hall.

> Mother to husband in son's presence: Jack, did you notice how Don put his bicycle in the garage tonight? He used to leave it out until we told him to put it away; he is becoming much more responsible, don't you think?

> Father to son: I appreciate your being quiet while I was figuring the income tax, son. You were very thoughtful. Now that I have that job done, I'll have more time. Why don't we plan to go to the zoo next Saturday?

> Teacher to high school student: You've made a good point, Juan. I hadn't thought of that aspect of the matter. I enjoy your original way of looking at things.

> Mother to small son: Kevin, you haven't sucked your thumb all morning. I'm very proud of you. Let's see how long you can go this afternoon.

It is unwise for a parent to compliment the child for behavior she does not admire. If everything the child does earns him a big hug and a pat on the back, Mom's approval gradually becomes meaningless. Inflation can destroy the value of her reinforcement. Specific behavior warranting genuine compliments can be found if it is sought, even in the most mischievous youngster.

3. Any behavior which is learned through reinforcement can be eliminated if the reward is withheld long enough

It is an absolute fact that unreinforced behavior will eventually disappear. This process, called *extinction* by psychologists, can be very useful to parents and teachers who want to alter the characteristics of children. The animal world provides many interesting examples of extinction; for example, the wall-eyed pike is a large fish with a big appetite for minnows. If he is placed in a tank of water with his small colleagues, he will soon be in the tank alone. However, an interesting thing occurs when a plate of glass is slipped down the middle of the tank, separating the pike from the minnows. The pike cannot see the glass, and he hits it solidly in pursuit of his dinner. Again and again he will swim into the glass, bumping whatever one calls the front end of a wall-eyed pike. His behavior is *not* being reinforced; it is gradually being extinguished. Eventually, the pike gives up in discouragement. He has learned that it is not possible to get the minnows. The glass can then be taken from the tank, allowing the minnows to swim around their mortal enemy in perfect safety. He will not try to eat them. He knows what he knows. They are unreachable. The wall-eyed pike will actually starve to death while his favorite food is bumping him on the gills and mouth.

Extinction is utilized to prevent circus elephants from throwing their mighty power against the restraining chain each evening. When the elephant is young, his foot is chained to a cement block that is totally immovable. He will pull repeatedly against the barrier without success, thereby extinguishing his escape behavior. Later, a small rope and a fragile stake will be sufficient to restrain the powerful elephant.

In order to eliminate an undesirable behavior, one must

identify and then withhold the critical reinforcement. Let's apply this principle to a common childhood problem: why does a child whine instead of speaking in a normal voice? Because the parent has reinforced whining! As long as three-year-old Karen is speaking in her usual voice, her mom is too busy to listen to her. Karen babbles all day long, anyway, so her mother tunes out most of her verbiage. But when Karen speaks in a grating, irritating, obnoxious tone, her mom turns to see what is wrong. Karen's whining brings results; her normal voice does not: she becomes a whiner. In order to extinguish the whining, one must merely reverse the reinforcement. Mom should begin by saying, "I can't hear you because you're whining, Karen. I have funny ears; they just can't hear whining." After this message has been passed along for a day or two, Mom should show no indication of having heard a moan-tone. She should then offer immediate attention to a request made in a normal voice. If this control of reinforcement is applied properly, I guarantee it to achieve the desired results. All learning is based on this principle, and the consequences are certain and definite. Of course, Grandma and Uncle Albert may continue to reinforce the behavior you are trying to extinguish, and they can keep it alive.

Teachers should know how to tame the classroom show-off in the same manner. First decide what is motivating his behavior: it takes no great scientist to recognize that the loudmouth is usually seeking the attention of the group. Some children had much rather be thought of as obnoxious than to be unthought of at all. For them, anonymity is the most painful experience imaginable. The ideal prescription is to extinguish their attention-getting behavior and then meet their need for gaining acceptance by less noisy means. I worked with a giddy little sixth grader named Larry whose mouth never shut. He perpetually disrupted the tranquility of his class, setting up a constant barrage of silliness, wise remarks and horseplay. His teacher and I constructed an isolated area in a remote corner of the schoolroom; from that spot he could see nothing but the front of the room. Thereafter, Larry was sentenced to a week in the isolation booth whenever he chose to be disruptive, which effectively eliminated the supporting reinforcement. Certainly, he could still act silly behind the screen, but he could not see the effect he was having on his peers. Besides this limitation, each outburst lengthened his lonely isolation. Larry spent one entire month in relative solitude before the extinction was finalized. When he rejoined society, his teacher immediately began to reward his cooperation. He was given the high status jobs, (messenger, sergeant-at-arms, etc.) and praised for the improvement he had made. The results were remarkable.

Some school districts have implemented a more structured form of extinction for their worst behavioral problems (that is, the behavior is extinguished, not the children!). The students who are seemingly incapable of classroom cooperation are assigned to special classes, consisting of twelve to fifteen students. These youngsters are then placed on a program called "systematic exclusion." The parents are informed that the only way their child can remain in a public school is for them to come and get him if they are called during the school day. The child is then told that he can come to school each morning, but the moment he breaks one of the well-defined rules, he will be sent home. He might be ejected for pushing other pupils in the line at 9:01 A.M. Or he may make it until 1:15 or later before dismissal occurs. There are no second chances, although the child is free to return at the start of school the following morning. Despite the traditional belief that children hate school, most of them hate staying home even more. Women's daytime television gets pretty monotonous, particularly under the hostile eye of a mom who had to interrupt her activities to come get her wayward son. Disruptive behavior is very quickly extinguished under this controlled setting. It just isn't profitable for the student to challenge the system. Positive reinforcement in the form of candy and other rewards is then generously applied for the child's attempts to learn and study. I worked with one child in a behavior modification classroom who was termed the most disruptive child ever seen at a major Los Angeles neuropsychiatric hospital. After four months in this controlled setting, he was able to attend a regular class in the public schools.

Extinction occasionally happens accidentally, as it did in the case of four-year-old Mark. His mother and father were concerned about his irritating habit of throwing temper tantrums. He would select the time when his parents least wanted him to misbehave; when guests were visiting in their home, he could be expected to explode at bedtime, if not before. Mark repeated the same emotional performance in restaurants, church services and other public places. His parents were no strangers to discipline, and they unloaded all their resources on their little rebel. They spanked him, stood him in the corner, sent him to bed early, shamed and scolded him. Nothing worked. The temper tantrums continued on a regular basis. Finally, they reached the point of exasperation. They didn't know what else to do. Then one evening Mark's parents were reading the newspaper in their living room. They had said something that angered him, and he fell on the floor in a rage. He screamed and whacked his head on the carpet, kicking, and flailing his small arms. They didn't know what to do with him, so they did nothing. They went on reading the paper. That reaction was totally unexpected by villainous Mark. He got up, looked at his father, and fell down for

Act II. Again his parents made no response. Mark's yelling stopped abruptly. He went over to his mother and shook
her arm, then collapsed for Act III. Still they made no
move toward him. He apparently felt so silly flopping alone
on the floor that he never threw another tantrum. In retro-
spect, it is clear that the reinforcement for Mark's tantrums
was parental manipulation. He was able to get those big,
powerful adults upset and distraught through this violent
behavior. Tantrums are more frequently a form of challenging behavior which can be eliminated by one or more appropriate spankings; for a few children, like Mark, the
spanking itself is actually a form of reinforcement. For
Mark, like the pyromaniac, it was rewarding to see how
much commotion he could precipitate.

Although Mark's parents extinguished his negative behavior in one episode, it usually takes much longer. It is
important to understand the typical rate at which a characteristic will disappear without reinforcement. Consider
again the example of the pigeon checking radio tubes. He
began the learning exercise by missing all the defective
tubes, gradually recognizing a higher and higher percentage.
As is illustrated in Figure A, the pigeon eventually identified
one hundred percent of the tubes, and he continued to
function with perfect accuracy as long as the reinforcement (grain) was paid for each success. Suppose the reinforcement was then withheld. The pigeon would continue to
intercept the defective parts with perfect accuracy, but not
for long. Soon he would begin to miss a few tubes. If he
continued to work for nothing, he would become more and
more distracted and disinterested in his task. By the end
of the day, he would miss all or most of the defective tubes.
However, the following day, he would again go to work as
before. *Even though the behavior is extinguished on one
day, it is likely to return the next.* This reawakening is

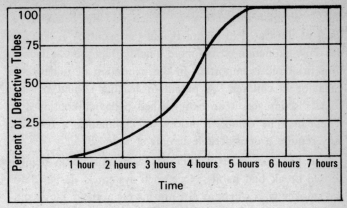

Figure A

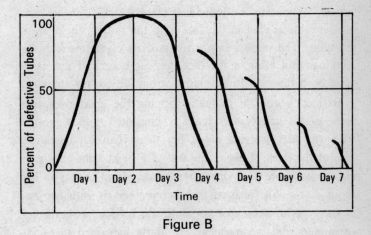

Figure B

called "spontaneous recovery." Each day the behavior re-
turns as illustrated in Figure B, but the accuracy is less and
the daily extinction occurs more quickly than the day before.
This principle is important in the extinction of undesirable
behavior in children. A parent or teacher should not become discouraged if an extinguished behavior continues to
reappear. The complete process of eliminating a response
may require a considerable period of time.

The principle of extinction has been utilized in helping
people break bad habits. One such system is designed for
the smoker who wants to give up his cigarettes. To accomplish the objective, his experimenters must eliminate the
pleasantness (reinforcement) usually produced by inhaling
cigarette smoke. A tube is aimed at the face of the smoker
from which will come very stale, concentrated tobacco
smoke. Whenever the individual takes a puff from his own
cigarette, he is shot in the face with the putrid smoke from
the tube. The smoker begins to associate cigarettes with the
stinking, foul blast in the face, and at least half the cases
have been reported to develop a strong dislike for smoking.

Extinction can be useful in helping the child overcome
some of his unnecessary fears. I consulted with a mother
who was very worried about her three-year-old daughter's
fear of the dark. Despite the use of a night light and leaving the bedroom door open, Marla was afraid to stay in her
room alone. She insisted that her mother sit with her until she went to sleep each evening, which became very time-
consuming and inconvenient. If Marla happened to awak-
en in the night, she would call for help. It was apparent that
the child was not bluffing; she was genuinely frightened.
Fears such as this are not innate characteristics in the child;
they have been learned. Parents must be very careful in expressing their fears, because their youngsters are amazingly

perceptive in adopting those same concerns. For that matter, good-natured teasing can also produce problems for a child. If a youngster walks into a dark room and is pounced upon from behind the door, he has learned something from the joke: the dark is not always empty! In Marla's case, it is unclear where she learned to fear the dark, but I believe her mother inadvertently magnified the problem. In her concern for Marla, she conveyed her anxiety, and Marla began to think that her fears must be justified. "Even mother is worried about it." The fright became so great that Marla could not walk through a dimly lit room without an escort. It was at this point that the child was referred to me. I suggested that the mother tell Marla she was going to help her see that there was nothing to be afraid of. (It is usually unfruitful to try to *talk* a child out of his fears but it helps to show him you are confident and unthreatened.) She bought a bag of candy and placed her chair just outside Marla's bedroom door. Marla was then offered a piece of candy if she could spend a short time (ten seconds) in her bedroom with the light on and the door shut. This first step was not very threatening, and Marla enjoyed the game. It was repeated several times; then she was asked to walk a few feet into the darkened room with the door open while mother (clearly visible in the hall) counted to ten. Marla accomplished this task several times and was given the candy on each occasion. On subsequent trips, the door was shut halfway, followed by a more narrow opening. Finally, Marla had the courage to enter the dark room and shut the door while her mother counted to ten. She knew she could come out immediately if she wished. Mother talked confidently and quietly. The length of time in the dark was gradually lengthened, and instead of producing fear, it produced candy: ultimate pleasure to a small child. Courage was being reinforced; fear was being extinguished. The cycle of fright was thereby broken, being replaced by a more healthy attitude.

The uses of extinction are limited only by the imagination and creativity of the parent or teacher. The best method of changing a behavior is to withhold its reinforcement while rewarding its replacement.

4. Parents and teachers are also vulnerable to reinforcement

Reinforcement is not only the mechanism by which children and animals learn new behavior; adults also modify their behavior according to their successes and failures. Not infrequently a child will train his parents, rather than the reverse, by reinforcing certain behaviors and extinguishing others. A few examples are described below:

When Mother and Father decide to take their children to some exciting place, such as Disneyland, the youngsters put on their best behavior. They are sweet and cooperative, in an unsubtle attempt to "reinforce" their parents' behavior. In extreme cases, I have seen children manipulate their parents in a cool application of reinforcement to the behavior they prefer.

When Mom disciplines her eight-year-old daughter, the child says, "You don't love me anymore." Most children know their parents are anxious to convey their love, so they use this delicate issue to extinguish punishment. It often succeeds.

When the teacher says, "It is time to study health, so get out your health books," the entire class groans "Oh, no!" For some teachers, this lack of reinforcement is very difficult to tolerate, and the subject of health is eliminated from their curriculum in the future. Similar phenomena occur in higher education too! I knew of a graduate school psychology class which was studying the principles of reinforcement, and the students decided to conduct an experiment involving their professor. Their instructor utilized two approaches to teaching: he would lecture from his notes, which proved to be a dry, dismal experience for the students. However, he was much more interesting when they could get him to talk extemporaneously, answering their questions and speaking from his wealth of knowledge. The students agreed before class one day to reward his free conversation and extinguish his formal lecturing behavior. Whenever he talked from his notes, they shuffled their feet, looked out the window, yawned and whispered to each other. On the other hand, they reflected maximum fascination with his unstructured lessons. The professor responded in classic fashion: Although he did not know he was being manipulated until near the end of the semester, he changed his mode of instruction in favor of the informal approach.

Father has a very low frustration tolerance with his children. Whenever they fall short of his expectations, he yells at them, which seems to make them mind. He has been reinforced for his screaming and becomes a loud, aggressive parent.

Adults even reinforce each other in regard to the subjects about which they will converse. For example, Marsha and Harry are talking but Harry is bored with the topic; for that matter, Harry is also bored with Marsha. His disinterest cannot be concealed. His boredom produces telltale yawns that defy suppression. They creep up Harry's throat and pound on his teeth until released. Harry waits until Marsha looks away, then he sets his jaw, swallows hard, and squeezes the yawn out his eyes. When Marsha looks at Harry again, she sees suspicious tears left by the compressed yawn. Marsha can hardly miss the other signs of boredom, including Harry's lack of involvement and his glazed appearance.

Perhaps without conscious awareness, Marsha knows she isn't impressing Harry; she may terminate the conversation as quickly as possible, or at least change the topic. Unless she is socially dead, she will decode and react to the lack of reinforcement Harry is providing. In a similar fashion, we "tell" each other what subjects we want to talk about.

The point of this section is simple: parents should be aware of their own reactions to reinforcement, and make certain they are in control of the new learning situation.

5. Parents often reinforce undesirable behavior and weaken the behavior they value

Perhaps the most important aspect of this chapter relates to accidental reinforcement. It is remarkably easy to reward undesirable behavior in children by allowing it to succeed. Suppose, for example, that Mr. and Mrs. Weakknee are having guests in for dinner tonight, and they put three-year-old Ricky to bed at 7:00 P.M. They know Ricky will cry, as he always does, but what else can they do? Indeed, Ricky cries. He begins at a low pitch (which does not succeed) and gradually builds to a high intensity scream. Finally, Mrs. Weakknee becomes so embarrassed by the display that she lets Ricky get up. What has the child learned? That he must cry loudly if he wants to get up. Mr. and Mrs. Weakknee had better be prepared for a tearful battle scene tomorrow night, too, because the method was successful to Ricky the night before.

Betty Sue is an argumentative teen-ager. She never takes "no" for an answer. She is very cantankerous; in fact, her father says the only time she is ever homesick is when she is at home. Whenever her mother is not sure about whether she wants to let Betty go to a party or ball game, she will first tell her she *can't* go. By saying an initial "no," Betty's mom doesn't commit herself to a "yes" before she's had a chance to think it over. She can always change her mind from negative to positive, but it is difficult to go the other way. However, what does this system tell Betty? She can see that "no" really means "maybe." The harder she argues and complains, the more likely she is to obtain the desired "yes." Many parents make the same mistake as Betty Sue's mother. They allow arguing, sulking, pouting, door-slamming, and bargaining to succeed. A parent should not take a definitive position on an issue until he has thought it over thoroughly. Then he should stick tenaciously to his stand. If the teen-ager learns that "no" means "absolutely no," he is less likely to waste his effort appealing his case to higher courts.

It is Mr. and Mrs. Smith's tenth wedding anniversary and they are going out for dinner. As they get ready to leave, their five- and six-year-old children begin to howl about being left behind. Mr. Smith is vaguely familiar with the principles of reinforcement, so he offers some candy to the children if they'll stop crying. Unfortunately, Mr. Smith has not reinforced the silence; he has rewarded the tears. The next time he and Mrs. Smith leave, it will be to the childrens' advantage to cry again. The tears are necessary to obtain the candy once more. A small alteration would have changed the setting, entirely. Mr. Smith should have offered the candy for their cooperation before the tears began to fall.

Seven-year-old Abe wants the attention of his family, and he knows of no constructive way to get it. At the dinner table one evening his mother says, "Eat your beans, Abe," to which he replies defiantly, "No! I won't eat those rotten beans!" He has the eyes and ears of the whole family — something he wanted in the first place. Abe's mother can solidify the success of his defiance (and guarantee its return) by saying, "If you'll eat your beans I'll give you a treat."

The crying of infants is an important form of communication. Through their tears we learn of their hunger, fatigue, discomfort, or diaper disaster. Although we do not want to eliminate crying in babies, it is possible to make them less fussy and tearful by minimizing the reinforcement of this behavior. If an infant is immediately picked up or rocked each time he cries, he may quickly observe the relationship between tears and adult attention. I have stood at the doorway of my daughter's nursery for four or five minutes, awaiting a momentary lull in the crying before going to her crib. By so doing, I reinforce the pauses rather than the emotional intensity.

Obviously, a parent must be careful in the behavior he allows to succeed. He must exercise self-discipline and patience to insure that the reinforcement which takes place is positive, not negative in its results. Here are some questions that have been asked, with my answers and suggestions.

QUESTIONS AND ANSWERS

1. You stated earlier that you do not favor spanking a teen-ager. What would you do to encourage the cooperation of my fourteen-year-old who deliberately makes a nuisance of himself? He throws his clothes around, refuses to help out with any routine tasks in the house, and pesters his little brother perpetually.

If he receives an allowance, this money could provide an excellent tool with which you can generate a little motivation. Suppose he is given two dollars a week. That maximum can be taxed regularly for violations of predetermined rules. For example, each article of clothing left on the floor might cost him a dime. A deliberate provocation of his brother would subtract a quarter from his total. Each Saturday, he would receive the amount of money remaining from the taxation of the last week. This system accomplishes the major objective shaping the behavior of a child: give him reason for obeying *other than* simply the fact that he was told to do so.

2. You gave a very specific example of how to get a five-year-old to carry responsibility. Can you describe in detail a similar technique for motivating a lazy teenager?

The principles of reinforcement are particularly useful with teen-agers, because rewards appeal to youngsters during this typically self-centered time of life. However, laziness is an unavoidable fact of life with many adolescents. Their lack of industriousness and general apathy have a physiological origin; energy is being redirected into rapid growth. Also, glandular changes require a physical readjustment. For several years they may want to sleep until noon and drag themselves around the rest of the day. If any system will succeed in charging their sluggish batteries, it will probably involve a reward of some variety.

The following steps can be followed in implementing a system of reinforcement with a sixteen-year-old. (1) *Decide what is important to the youngster for use as an incentive.* Two hours with the family car on a date night is worth all manner of effort to most newly licensed drivers. (This could prove to be the most expensive incentive in history if the young driver is a bit shaky behind the wheel.) An allowance is another easily available source of motivation as described above. In this affluent day, teen-age boys have a great need for cold cash; a routine date with Helen

Highschool may cost him twenty dollars or more. A third
incentive may involve a fashionable article of clothing which
would not ordinarily be purchased. Offering the teen-ager a
means of obtaining such luxuries is a happy alternative to
the whining, crying, begging, complaining, and pestering
that would occur otherwise. Mom says, "Sure you can have
the ski sweater, but you'll have to earn it." Once an acceptable motivator is agreed upon, the second step is in order.
(2) *Formalize the agreement.* An excellent means of ac-
complishing this objective is use of a "contract." A written
statement is outlined, and the parent and the adolescent
both sign it. A point system is often agreed upon which
will lead to the goal in a reasonable period of time. A
period of negotiation may be necessary with binding arbi-
tration provided by an outside party. Let's examine a typical
agreement: Marshall wants a cassette tape recorder; he can
use it to play musical tapes, record lectures in the classroom
(an unlikely objective), and play it at parties and social
gatherings. His birthday is ten months away and he is flat
broke. The cost of the recorder he wants is approximately
forty dollars. His father agrees to buy the device if Marshall
will earn 10,000 points which may take six to ten weeks to
earn. There may be dozens of ways he can earn points;
many of those opportunities are delineated in advance,
but the list can be lengthened as other possibilities become
apparent:

1. For making bed and straightening
   room each morning _____ 50 points
2. For each hour of studying_____150 points
3. For each hour of house or yard work done 300 points
4. For being on time at meals, morning
   and night _____ 40 points
5. For baby-sitting with younger siblings
   (per hour) _____150 points
6. For washing car each week_____250 points

  7. For arising by 8:00 A.M. on
     Saturday morning _____100 points

The parent's imagination will supply other chores!

Just as Marshall can gain points for his cooperation, he can
lose them for resistance. Disagreeable and unreasonable
behavior can be penalized 50 points or more. (However,
penalties must be imposed fairly or the entire system will
crumble.) Bonus points can be awarded for behavior that
is particularly commendable. (3) *The third step in this system involves the establishment of a method to provide immediate rewards.* This is necessary to sustain the teen-ager's
interest as he moves toward the ultimate goal. A chart de-
picting a thermometer can be constructed, with the point
scale listed down the side. At the top is the 10,000 point
mark, with a picture of a cassette recorder resting at the
peak. Each evening, the daily points are totalled and the
red portion of the thermometer is extended upward. If
Marshall changes his mind about the purchase he wishes to
make, the points can be diverted to a new objective; (5,-
000 points is 50 percent of 10,000 and would be worth twenty dollars toward another goal.) It is most important that
the teen-ager not be given the goal if he does not earn it.
That practice would eliminate future uses of the reinforcement technique. Likewise, it would be unwise to deny or
postpone the goal once it is earned.

  The system described above is not absolute. It must be
adapted to the age and maturity of the adolescent. One
youngster would be insulted by an approach that would
thrill another. The principles are almost universally effective; the method of application must be varied.

  3. Can rewards be employed in a church or Sunday school
     program?

I have seen reinforcement utilized with great effectiveness in a Christian Sunday school. Instead of earning money, the children were able to accumulate "talents," which resembled toy money of various denominations. (The concept of talents was taken from Jesus' parable of the talents in the New Testament.) The children earned talents by learning memory verses from Scripture, being punctual on Sunday morning, having perfect attendance, bringing a visitor, and so on. This system of currency was then used to "purchase" new items from those on display in a glass case. Bibles, fountain pens, books, puzzles, and other religious or educational prizes were available for selection. The children's division blossomed in the church where this system was employed. There may be those who would oppose this materialistic program in a church setting, and that is a matter for individual evaluation.

4. I have two boys who are two years apart in age; one is seven and the other is nine. They never stop fighting and arguing. What should I do about this?

Conflict between siblings is as natural as eating and sleeping. In fact, it could almost be considered unnatural for them to coexist in constant harmony, although that does occur occasionally. I don't believe you should be concerned about the routine bickering that you hear, even if it breaks into open warfare at times. On the other hand, your intervention might be needed if you begin to see symptoms of greater difficulty. It is important to verify that one child, usually the younger, is not constantly losing in those battles. An older child can make life miserable for his weaker rival. When this is happening, the parent should use his influence to reestablish a balance of power. A younger child can sometimes be equally antagonistic. He may confiscate or destroy all the prized possessions of his older sibling, or make an unbearable nuisance of himself. Thus, when one child is the definite aggressor and the other is showing signs of considerable frustration, parental intervention is in order. But I would suggest that you ignore the less significant conflicts, allowing the youngsters to fight their own battles.

Even though there is no great psychological meaning to routine sibling bickering, I can offer two suggestions which may reduce the noise level of your home.

(1) Offer a tangible reward to the boys for each day they can survive without a fuss or a fight. Perhaps they could each be offered a dime a day if they can avoid conflict. If one child quietly refuses to respond to an attack by the other, only he will receive the reward that evening. (2) Sibling rivalry is often centered around the issue of privileges at home. These can be balanced by the parent. There are some things an older child gets to do because he is older (stay up later, go more places, etc.). There are other privileges which favor the position of the younger child (he gets his choice of toys, he has less work to do, etc.). The wise parent will convince her children that she is trying to be fair in this regard.

5. Should parents force a child to eat?

No. I am not an expert in nutrition, but I believe a child's appetite is governed by the amount of food he needs. He will get hungry when he needs nourishment. However, I do believe the parent should carefully guard that appetite, making sure that he satisfies it with the foods his body requires. A little bit of sugar in the afternoon can make him disinterested in his dinner. Or he may sit down at the table and fill his stomach with juice or one item on his plate. It may be necessary to give him one kind of food at a time, beginning with iron-rich meat and other protein, followed by the less important items. Once he is satisfied, I can see no value in forcing him to continue eating. Incidentally, the parent should know that a child's appetite often drops off rapidly between two and three years of age. This occurs because his time of maximum growth has subsided, and his need for food is reduced.

6. I am a teacher in junior high school, and there are five separate classes that come to my room to be taught science each day. My biggest problem is getting these students to bring books, paper and pencils to class with them. I can lend them the equipment they need, but I never get it back. What do you suggest?

I faced an identical problem the year I taught in junior high school. My students were not malicious; they just had too many other things on their minds to remember to bring their school materials. I tried various techniques for motivation on this issue, but without success. I appealed to the students for assistance with this problem but I couldn't stir up an ounce of enthusiasm. I went through an emotional tirade, but that seemed like a great waste of energy for such a small issue. There had to be a better way! I finally reached a solution which is based on the certainty that young people will cooperate if it is to their advantage to do so. I announced one morning that I was no longer concerned about whether they brought their pencils and books to class. I had twenty extra books and several boxes of sharpened pencils which they could borrow. If they forgot to bring these materials, all they had to do was ask for a loan. I would not gnash my teeth or get red in the face; they would find me very willing to share my resources. However, there was to be one hitch: the borrowing student would have to forfeit his seat for that one-hour class. He would have to stand by his chair while I was teaching, and if any written work was required, he had to lean over his desk from a standing position. As might be imagined, the students were less than ecstatic about this prospect. I smiled to myself as I saw them racing around before class, trying to borrow a book or pencil. I did not have to enforce the standing rule very often because the issue had become the pupils' campaign rather than mine. Once a week, or so, a student would have to spend the hour in a vertical position, but that youngster made certain he did not blunder into the same situation twice.

At the risk of being unnecessarily redundant, I will repeat the valuable formula for controlling children: give them maximum reason to comply with your wishes. Your anger is the *least* effective motivation I can imagine.

III

Discipline in the Classroom

"READING, WRITING, AND ARITHMETIC, LOST FOR THE WANT OF A HICKORY STICK"

It should now be apparent to everyone that we are in the midst of a very serious worldwide revolution. This cataclysmic social upheaval is being ignited and fueled by the young — the students — the "under thirty" populace. Whether they be in Tokyo, Paris, London, or on the campuses of American universities, these antagonists are united in their opposition to one common target: authority in all its forms. Every institution of authority is now being challenged: the police, the military, the Catholic Church, the Protestant Church, the family, the courts, the high schools, the universities, the FBI, the CIA, and the mores and values of society itself. Even in medical school, which has been the traditional stronghold of discipline and rigor, students are becoming more militant and defiant. No young person wants to be "told" anything by his superiors — assuming that he recognizes his superiors at all. This hostility in the new generation reaches its peak in the minority of young revo-

lutionaries who want to burn and destroy the holdings of
the establishment. They have no program of reform; their
platform includes nothing but universal destruction — in
the vain hope that something better will follow. Students
for a Democratic Society (SDS) and similar organizations
have initiated open conflict on more than two hundred university campuses, and their activity is equally alarming at
the high school level. These young militants are angry because America has the audacity to be imperfect, and they
wish to annihilate its leaders and institutions. Unfortunately,
they underestimate the vital function of authority in a civilization. Respect for leadership is the glue that holds social or-
ganization together. Without it there is chaos, violence, and
insecurity for everyone. It seems likely that the world is
destined to learn this painful lesson once more.

In the first chapter of this book, I discussed the *primary*
cause of this pervasive disrespect for authority: parents in
the western world generally failed to instill responsible attitudes when their children were small. However, parents
should not be credited with the full blame; they have had
considerable assistance. The second most influential force
in the rise of disorder has been the school. Parents gave their
children a distorted view of authority, and the school glibly
seconded the motion. If the trend toward social chaos is to
be reversed, educators must cooperate with parents in
bringing about a revival of effective discipline in the classroom.

LACK OF CONTROL

During my early years of teaching experience, I was surprised to see the lack of order and control in many classrooms. The confusion was apparent at all age levels. Tiny

first grade children cowed their harassed teachers as systematically as did the boisterous high school students. In some situations, entire classes became so proficient at disrupting order that they were dreaded and feared by their future teachers. It seemed ridiculous for school officials to tolerate such disobedience when it could have been easily eliminated. However, in those instances when the educators did exercise firmness, many parents protested and demanded leniency for their children. Later, we began to observe the behavioral consequences of this lack of discipline. For example, I had the enlightening responsibility of serving as a counselor for 450 disrespectful, haughty ninth graders. They marched into high school with clenched fists. They were proud of their academic failure. They were sullen, profane, and unappreciative. Even then, in 1963, it was estimated that one-third of these middle-class students were using narcotics of some kind. They were the forerunners of the hostile, aggressive, drug-using teen-agers seen in many high schools today.

From the perspective of those years, it was apparent that greater social troubles were on the horizon. I shared the concern of the famous criminologists, Professor and Mrs. Sheldon Glueck,* as reflected in an interview which was published in *U. S. News and World Report,* April, 1965. Their responses to the following questions have proved to be quite prophetic:

Question: *What seems to be causing delinquency to grow so fast nowadays?*

Answer: There are many causes for this. For the most part, however, what we are seeing now is a pro-

---

*Professor and Mrs. Glueck are most noted for their longitudinal study of juvenile delinquency and its causes.

cess that has been going on since the second
World War.

First, you have more and more mothers going
to work. Many have left their children more or
less unattended, at home or on the streets. This
has deprived children of the constant guidance
and sense of security they need from their mothers
in their early years.

Along with that change, parental attitudes toward disciplining their young have changed quite
rapidly. In the home and outside, the trend has
been steadily toward more permissiveness — that
is, placing fewer restraints and limits on behavior.

Question: *How has that philosophy worked out in practice?*

Answer: Not very well, it seems. Life requires a certain
amount of discipline. You need it in the classroom, you need it in the home, you need it in
society at large. After all, the Ten Commandments impose a discipline. *Unless general restraints are built into the character of children,
you can arrive eventually at social chaos.*

Question: *Are you saying that moral values are crumbling?*
(Author's note: This question preceded the "new
morality" by several years.)

Answer: This is part of the picture. Not only parents, but
others are uncertain in many cases as to what is
morally right or wrong, and that makes discipline
harder to enforce.

For instance, children today are being exposed
to all kinds of moving pictures and books. It is
difficult to decide what moving pictures and books

should be censored.

In a broad sense, actually, you might feel that censorship in general is undesirable. Yet you also know that restraint must be imposed at some point — especially where children are involved. But in trying to decide at what point restraint should be imposed, it very often turns out that no restraint at all results. And it is this lack of restraint in the home and on the outside that is back of so much of our delinquency.

Question: *Do juvenile courts tend to be too soft on youngsters?*

Answer: Sometimes, yes, but more often there is inconsistency because judges have wide discretion; and they may rely on intuition and hunches rather than the use of predictive data which their staff could gather for them on each case.

Question: *Then is stern punishment a deterrent to further crime?*

Answer: Certainty of punishment is definitely a deterrent. After all, fear is a primary emotion in man. It plays an important part in his training. We have gone rather far in the other direction, in letting the child feel that he isn't going to be punished for his misdeeds.

Of course, it is wrong to rely exclusively on fear of punishment, but it is equally wrong to do away with this deterrent.

Question: *Can schools help in keeping children from developing into troublemakers?*

Answer: They certainly can. As we have said, there are
            children whose energies are not suited to long
            periods of sitting still and whose adventuresome-
            ness has to be satisfied in some acceptable way.

            We also think that one of the basic needs of
            schools, along with other elements of society, is
            a general recognition that rules must be observed
            — that, without rules, you drift into chaos and
            tyranny and into taking the law into your own
            hands. You see it not only among delinquents,
            but among young college students, in their de-
            mand for more and more freedom from restraints
            and from higher authority.

Question: *Do you look for crime and delinquency to grow?*

Answer: Probably. Our own feeling is that, unless much
            is done to check the vicious cycles involved, we
            are in for a period of violence beyond anything
            we have yet seen.

            All you have to do is to read about the mur-
            ders and assaults taking place in New York sub-
            ways. Only a few years ago nobody thought of
            public conveyances as being unsafe. We foresee
            no letup in this trend. A delinquent child often
            grows up to produce delinquent children — not
            as a matter of heredity, but of his own unresolved
            conflicts which make him an ineffective parent.

Professor and Mrs. Glueck clearly anticipated the anarchy which is now rumbling ominously from within the mid-
section of democracy. Nowhere is the danger more apparent than in the large city junior and senior high schools. A
teacher friend of mine recently told me he is looking for a
new line of work. He wants to leave the teaching profession because he is fearful for his safety, despite the fact that

he is a 6-foot 5-inch, 220-pound athlete. The students at his school have displayed more and more boldness in their physical confrontation with teachers. For example, a few weeks ago a student put a shotgun against the stomach of a faculty member and demanded the keys to his car. The teacher recognized the boy and thought he was joking; he pushed the gun aside. Again the student pointed his weapon at the teacher and threatened to shoot him if the keys were not delivered. The teacher refused to take the adolescent seriously, and went on his way. He was told later by investigating officers that he was lucky to be alive. So many teen-agers are using drugs now that their rationality cannot be presupposed. The epidemic of heroin addiction, which is already upon us, has resulted in numerous panic-stricken young people who are driven to reduce their inner torment. Everyone near them must share their peril.

The degree of student control exercised by school authorities has never been so minimal as it is today in America. Some concerned parents are refusing to send their children to school until student safety can be guaranteed. We simply must restore a greater semblance of order in our junior and senior high schools, yet the trend at this time is toward more and more student autonomy. Educational discipline is still on the wane, as is reflected in the elimination of traditional rules and regulations. Dress codes are being dropped, allowing students to wear the sloppiest, most distracting or suggestive clothing possible. Guidelines concerning hair length and good grooming are also being eliminated. While I agree with the viewpoint that hair style and similar matters of momentary fashion are not worthy of concern, in themselves, *adherence to a standard is an important element of discipline*. It is a great mistake to require *nothing* of children — to place no demands on their behavior. Whether a high school girl wears slacks or a dress is

not of earthshaking importance, although it *is* significant
that she be required to adhere to a few reasonable rules.
If one examines the secret behind a championship football
team, a magnificent orchestra, or a successful business, the
principal ingredient is invariably discipline. How inaccu-
rate is the belief that self-control is maximized in an environment which places no obligations on its children. How
foolish is the assumption that self-discipline is a product of
self-indulgence. How unfortunate has been the systematic
undermining of educational rules, engineered by a minority
of parents through the legal assistance of the American
Civil Liberties Union and the tired old judges to whom they
have appealed. Despite the will of the majority, the antidisciplinarians have had their way. The rules governing
student conduct have been cut down, and in their place have
come a myriad of restrictions on educators. School prayers
are illegal even if addressed to an unidentified God. The
Bible can be read only as uninspired literature. Allegiance
to the flag of our country cannot be required. Educators
find it very difficult to punish or expel a student. Teachers are
so conscious of parental militancy that they often withdraw
from the defiant challenges of their students. As a result,
academic discipline lies at the point of death in the nation's
schools.

Several years ago, it became fashionable in one American
city for students to boycott their classrooms in mass numbers. The same pattern was repeated throughout the area
for several weeks, characteristic of adolescent "bandwagon"
behavior. I investigated the details of one such boycott
which was typical of the others. The conflict was originated
by known troublemakers — a small band of students which
resorted to continual antagonism as a means of bringing
disruption. These students conferred at lunch time and
decided they didn't want to go to school that afternoon. Sev-

eral methods of "cutting" class were proposed; the suggestion was finally made that they stage a boycott. The word was passed around and several hundred students were recruited on the athletic field. A noisy rally ensued, producing a list of demands for presentation to the administrator. One young fellow was then sent to call the local newspaper, which responded by sending several camera-laden reporters and a mobile television van. It was the most exciting and successful venture the young militants had ever concocted — certainly more fun than sitting in history or English or general math classes. They felt like brave leaders of the oppressed masses, as they denounced members of the faculty and administration for their tyranny. The school principal reacted calmly and rationally. Whether or not the students' demands were valid was of little consequence; he wisely refused to negotiate at gunpoint. He warned that students who were not in class within the hour would be punished; about half the pupils returned to school, while the rest held out for noble reforms. After the riot had been quelled, the principal began taking the disciplinary action he had promised for the boycotting students. Before he could act, however, he received an order from the superintendent of the school district, instructing him to grant amnesty to all participants and to attempt to meet the demands presented by the students. At that moment, destiny chalked up another victory for violence and disorder. The young antagonists had found the experience to be stimulating and profitable. And they were given every reason to repeat the performance with greater vigor in the future. There is obvious danger involved in rewarding this kind of vigilante behavior by students. Once it succeeds, defiance becomes the logical recourse whenever the adolescents disagree with an administrative decision. Since educators will never be able to please all their students on every issue, violence is certain to recur, resulting in a kind of learning for which the school was never intended.

DISCIPLINE IN ELEMENTARY SCHOOL

Having established the importance of discipline in education, we must now focus our attention on how this objective can best be realized. In that regard, the ideal model for the school is provided by the home. Discipline in the child's early experiences begins with the fundamental relationship between his parents and himself, (particularly his mother); likewise, educational discipline should begin with the crucial interaction between a primary or elementary teacher and her students. As the first official voice of the school, the primary teacher is in a position to construct positive attitudinal foundations on which future educators can build, or conversely, she can fill her young pupils with contempt and disrespect. A child's first six teachers will largely determine the nature of his attitude toward authority in junior and senior high school (and beyond).

I taught school for several years before completing my graduate training, and learned more about how children think from that daily exposure than could ever have been assimilated from a textbook. It was also educational to observe the disciplinary techniques utilized by other teachers. Some of them exercised perfect classroom control with little effort, while others faced the perpetual humiliation of student defiance. I observed that there was a fundamental difference in the way they approached their classes. The unskilled teacher would stand in front of the boys and girls and immediately seek their affection. Although most good teachers want to be liked by their classes, some are very dependent on the acceptance of the children. On the first day of school in September, the new teacher, Miss Peach, gives the class a little talk which conveys this message: "I'm so glad we had a chance to get together. This is going to be such a fun year for you; we're going to make soap, and soup, and we're going to paint a mural that will cover that entire wall. We'll take field trips and play games . . . this is going to be a great year. You're going to love me and I'm going to love you, and we'll just have a ball." Her curriculum is well saturated with fun, fun, fun activities, which are her tokens of affection to the class. All goes well the first day of school, because the students are a little intimidated by the start of a new academic year. But about three days later, little Butch is sitting over at the left, and he wants to know what everyone else is questioning, too: how far can we push Miss Peach? He is anxious to make a name for himself as a brave toughie, and he might be able to build his reputation at Miss Peach's expense. At a well-calculated moment, he challenges her with a small act of defiance. Now the last thing Miss Peach wants is conflict, because she had hoped to avoid that sort of thing this year. She does not accept Butch's challenge; she pretends not to notice that he didn't do what she told him to do. He wins this first minor issue. Everyone in the class saw what happened; it wasn't a big deal, but Butch survived unscathed. The next day, Matthew has been greatly encouraged by Butch's success. Shortly after the morning flag salute, he defies her a little more openly than Butch did, and Miss Peach again ignores the challenge. From that moment forward, chaos begins to grow and intensify. Two weeks later Miss Peach is beginning to notice that things are not going very well. She's doing a lot of screaming each day and she doesn't know how it got started; she certainly didn't intend to be a violent teacher. By February, life has become intolerable in her classroom; every new project she initiates is sabotaged by her lack of control. And then the thing she wanted least begins to happen: the students openly reveal their hatred and contempt for her. They call her names; they laugh at her weaknesses. If she has a physical flaw, such as a large nose or poor eyesight, they point this out to her regularly. Miss Peach cries quietly at recess time, and her head throbs and pounds late into the night. The principal comes in and witnesses the anarchy, and he says, "Miss Peach, you must get control of this class!" But Miss Peach doesn't know *how* to get control because she doesn't know how she lost it.

It has been estimated that 80 percent of the teachers who quit their jobs after the first year do so because of an inability to maintain discipline in their classroom. Do the colleges and teacher training programs respond to this need by offering specific courses in methods of control? No! Do the State Legislatures require formal coursework to help teachers handle this first prerequisite to teaching? No, despite the fact that learning is impossible in a chaotic classroom!

Consider the contrasting approach of the skillful teacher, Mrs. Justice. She wants the love of the class too, but she is more keenly aware of her responsibility to the students. On the first day of school she delivers her inaugural address, but it is very different from the one being spoken by Miss Peach. She says, in effect, "This is going to be a good year, and I'm glad you are my students. I want you to know that each one of you is important to me. I hope you will feel free to ask your questions, and enjoy learning in this class; I will not allow anyone to laugh at you, because it hurts to be laughed at. I will never embarrass you intentionally, and I want to be your friend. But there's one thing you should know: if you choose to challenge me I have one thousand ways to make you miserable. If you don't believe me, you just let me know and we'll start with number one. Your parents have given me the responsibility of teaching you some very important things this year, and I have to get you ready for the knowledge you will learn next year. That's why I can't let one or two show-offs keep me from doing my job. We have a lot to learn, so I think we'd better get started. Please get out your math books and turn to page four." About three days later, Butch's counter-part is on the job. (There's at least one Butch in every class-room; if the classroom antagonist leaves during the year, a new demagogue will emerge to prominence.) He challenges Mrs. Justice in a cautious manner, and she socks it to him. He loses big! Everyone in the class gets the message: it doesn't pay to attack Mrs. J. Wow! This poor Butch didn't do so well, did he? Mrs. Justice then proceeds to follow a little formula that I favor (tongue in cheek): *don't smile 'till Thanksgiving.* By November, this competent teacher has made her point. The class knows she's tougher, wiser, and braver than they are. Then she can begin to enjoy the pleasure of this foundation. She can loosen her control; the class can laugh together, talk together and play together. But when Mrs. Justice says, "It is time to get back to work," they do it because they know she is capable of enforcing her suggestion. She does not scream. She does not hit. In fact, she can pour out the individual affection that most children need so badly. The class responds with deep love that will never be forgotten in those thirty-two lives. Mrs. Justice has harvested the greatest source of satisfaction available in the teaching profession: awareness of profound influence on human lives.

SCHOOLS WITHOUT DISCIPLINE

Not everyone recognizes the importance of control in the classroom. In a widely publicized book entitled *Summerhill,* the author, A. S. Neill, describes his supervision of an English school where discipline is virtually nonexistent. The resident students at Summerhill are not required to get out of bed in the morning, or attend classes, complete assignments, take baths, or even wear clothes. Neill's philosophy is the antithesis of everything I have found worthwhile in the training of children; his misunderstanding of discipline and authority is complete and absolute. His brand of permissive absurdity gave birth to the social disasters we now face with our young. Listed below are the elements of Neill's philosophy which are particularly incriminating.

1. Adults, says Neill, have no right to insist on obedience from their children. Attempts to make the youngsters obey are merely designed to satisfy the adult's desire for power. There is no excuse for imposing parental wishes on children. They must be free. The best home situation is one where parents and children are perfect equals. A child should be required to do nothing until he *chooses* to do so. (This viewpoint is implemented at Summerhill, where the complete absence of authority is evident. Neill goes to great lengths to show the students that he is one of them — not their superior.)

2. Children must not be asked to work at all until they reach eighteen years of age. Parents should not even require them to help with small errands or assist with the chores. We insult them by making them do our menial tasks; Neill actually stressed the importance of withholding responsibility from the child.

3. Religion should not be taught to children. The only reason religion exists in society is to release the false guilt it has generated over sexual matters. Our concepts of God, heaven, hell, and sin are based on myths. En-

lightened generations of the future will reject traditional religion.

4. Punishment of any kind is strictly forbidden according to Neill's philosophy. A parent who spanks his child actually hates him, and his desire to hurt the child results from his own unsatisfied sex life. At Summerhill, one young student broke seventeen windows without receiving so much as a verbal reprimand.

5. Adolescents should be told sexual promiscuity is not a moral issue at all. At Summerhill, premarital intercourse is not sanctioned only because Neill fears the consequences of public indignation. He and members of his staff have gone nude to eliminate sexual curiosity. He predicted that the adolescents of tomorrow would find a more healthy existence through an unrestricted sex life.

6. No pornographic books or materials should be withheld from the child. Neill indicated that he would buy filthy literature for any of his students who wished to have it. This, he feels, would cure their prurient interests — without harming the child.

7. Children should not be required to say "thank you" or "please" to their parents. Further, they should not even be *encouraged* to do so.

8. Rewarding a child for good behavior is a degrading and demoralizing practice. It is an unfair form of coercion.

9. Neill considers books to be insignificant in a school. Education should consist largely of work with clay, paint, tools, and various forms of drama. Learning is not without value, but it should come after play.

10. Even if a child fails in school, the matter should never be mentioned by his parents. The child's activities are strictly his business.

11. Neill's philosophy, in brief, is as follows: eliminate all authority; let the child grow without outside interference; don't instruct him; don't force anything on him.

If A. S. Neill had been the only proponent of this destructive viewpoint, it would not have been worthy of our concern. To the contrary, he represents an entire era, dominated by the neo-Freudians who reigned during the 1950s and early 1960s. The painful impact of those years will not soon fade. Most of the values held tightly by the "now" generation were implanted during the period I have described; please note how many of the following elements of the new morality can be traced to the permissive viewpoint represented by Neill: God is dead; immorality is wonderful; nudity is noble; irresponsibility is groovy; disrespect and irreverence are fashionable; unpopular laws are to be disobeyed; violence is an acceptable vehicle for bringing change (as were childhood tantrums); authority is evil; everyone over thirty is stupid; pleasure is paramount; diligence is distasteful. These beliefs have been the direct contribution of the antidisciplinarians who delicately fused an enormous timebomb in the generation they controlled. The relationship between permissive philosophies and adolescent militancy is too striking to be coincidental. Passive young people did not suddenly become violent. Self-centered petulance did not erupt spontaneously in America's young adults; it was cultivated and nurtured through the excesses and indulgences of the tender years. Selfishness, greed, impatience, and irresponsibility were allowed to flower and bloom in the name of childhood "freedom." This great misguided movement was perhaps the most unsuccessful social experiment in history, and yet its influence is still far from dead in our schools and homes.

The mistakes of the past are interesting only to the degree that they help us explain the present and preserve the future. Rather than bemoan the errors of yesterday, our greater concern is with the problem as it has evolved today. Specifically, the undisciplined generation has now reached high school and college age, and it is threatening to destroy America's educational system. School administrators must decide what they will do in response to rioting and civil disobedience. Like Miss Peach, they can deny they have been challenged in the hopes that their tormentors will tiptoe away, but that is a dangerous posture to assume. They can stick their heads in the sand, but that leaves a very vulnerable part of their anatomy exposed.

Administrators must admit the obvious reality that young militants are seeking revolution — not reform. The small percentage of hard-core revolutionaries is disinterested in bringing change through negotiation. They are after a bigger prize. Their motivation is derived from something more basic than the draft, Vietnam, war research, pollution, the voting age, police brutality, campus military recruitment, and so on. As Yippie leader Jerry Rubin has said, "Satisfy our demands and we lose." The real motive in campus violence is the electrifying grab for power and publicity. Obviously, the first goal in this campaign is to bring the great universities and other American institutions to their knees. Such organizations as Students for a Democratic Society make use of noble causes to enlist the cooperation of their less militant colleagues. Their grievances are merely ploys around which to generate emotion. Thus, it is naïve to think that settlement of inflated disagreements will eliminate conflict and strife. FBI Director J. Edgar Hoover is under no illusion as to the desires of the campus revolutionaries. He recently described the motives of the New Left to a Congressional committee in this manner: "At the center of the movement is an almost passionate desire to destroy, to annihilate, to tear down . . . to put it bluntly, they are subversive and the danger is great."

A PRESCRIPTION FOR ADMINISTRATORS

High school and college administrators can quell the floodtide of anarchy, provided they have the courage to face the threat squarely and firmly. Listed below are the measures which could help restore order and discipline on America's campuses:

1. *It should be unprofitable for students to riot and destroy.* This objective could easily be accomplished by use of a simple financial incentive. Every college student could be required to post a $5,000 bond at the beginning of the term in September. The cost of the bond would be approximately fifty dollars to the student, which is a nominal fee in comparison with today's educational expenses. If the student became involved in any destructive behavior during the term, the $5,000 would be forfeited to the university. The bonding company would then hound the young militant the rest of his life to retrieve their money. Most students would be less likely to burn a building, for example, if they knew they would help pay for its reconstruction. At least this procedure would separate the serious revolutionary from the student who merely wants a little excitement.

2. *Administrators should suspend or expel the active rioters.* Why are administrators so reluctant to eliminate their troublemakers? It should be remembered that thousands of students were denied acceptance to the large universities in favor of those who were admitted. If those fortunate students do not value the positions they were generously granted, more appreciative hopefuls are waiting to take them. Particularly in the state universities being supported by public funds, there should be certain obligations on the recipients of a free education. There is no justifiable reason for my tax money to be used to "educate" a student who seeks to destroy everything I value — including me! Amnesty should not be granted. In the event of a campus riot, national guard troops or security police should sur-

round the students, offering to let anyone leave the circle within a few minutes' time. Notification should be given to the rioters that *every* student remaining will be arrested, expelled, and prosecuted to the fullest extent of the law. If eight hundred students or more were sent home to dad, rioting might become less fashionable at good old Ivy U.

3. *State legislatures should set a very stiff penalty to be imposed on any nonstudent convicted of trespassing on high school or university campuses for the purpose of initiating disorder.* There is no acceptable reason for our tolerating the migrating militants!

4. *Students for a Democratic Society and all similar revolutionary organizations should be banned from American campuses.* The constitutional right of free speech was never intended to be the tool of such groups, having the avowed purpose of overthrowing our government by force. Freedom of speech can be preserved without allowing it to shield insurrection. The Constitution of the United States was written according to a principle called the "Social Contract," which is not often mentioned today. The social contract is the agreement whereby citizens of a democracy forfeit their right to exploit other citizens. They cannot kill, cheat, or defame each other. By sacrificing this ultimate "freedom," they gain security and protection for themselves. It would appear that the current demands in the name of freedom are in violation of this social contract.

5. *An effective mechanism should be established for evaluating legitimate student grievances.* This mechanism should be emphasized and used. When orderly attempts are made to bring about change, administrators should listen and respond to student opinions — they should be openminded without letting their brains leak out. However, under no circumstances should negotiation occur under duress or during times of premeditated conflict.

6. *Faculty members encouraging revolution should be dismissed.* Teachers and students should be free to express their dissent, but that freedom does not entitle them to foment violence.

These recommendations are designed to help relieve the threat to higher education in America. It is still possible to extinguish the fire at this time, although the conflagration is spreading. Violence is contagious and self-perpetuating. An effective demagogue could appear on the political scene, capable of mobilizing the seething hostility and resentment. Perhaps we will act in time.

Al Capp, the cartoonist-creator of Lil' Abner, recently left no doubts about his attitude toward campus militants and the indecisive administrators who protect them. He was offered $800 honorarium to speak to the students at Princeton University but he declined. In a letter to the president of the Princeton debating society, Capp is reported to have explained that his minimum fee was $3,500 plus $1,000 "combat pay" required for all Ivy League schools. Dissenters have been so violent during his recent engagements that he accused Princeton of training "subhumans."

SUMMARY

We have discussed the lack of discipline and control in America's schools, which has paralleled the decline in parental authority at home. Educators, like parents, were led to believe that children would thrive best in an atmosphere of complete freedom — even if that freedom encouraged the children to be selfish, irresponsible, demanding, discourteous, irreverent, and destructive. This ridiculous philosophy led Junior to the obvious conclusion that he was his own boss. He knew he was unmanageable, either at home or at school. It should have been possible to predict the attitudinal outcome of this freewheeling approach to child rearing. It seems highly probable that the present antagonism among the young is directly correlated with what was taught to them as children, and we must reckon with the antisocial consequences — which may include a revolution.

The Bible speaks of an unruly generation which would eventually come on the earth.

> "For people will love only themselves and their money; they will be proud and boastful, sneering at God, disobedient to their parents, ungrateful to them, and thoroughly bad. They will be hardheaded and never give in to others; they will be constant liars and trouble-makers and will think nothing of immorality. They will be rough and cruel, and sneer at those who try to be good. They will betray their friends; they will be hot-headed, puffed up with pride, and prefer good times to worshiping God. They will go to church, yes, but they won't really believe anything they hear."

If we have not yet arrived at this degenerate point, we certainly appear to be moving in that direction.

How can we teach constructive attitudes to a generation of young people which is no longer listening to our advice? We can't. We must direct our attention toward the next generation of Americans — the children who are still pliable to guidance and training. Not only must we reinstate discipline at home (the first obligation) but the authority of the school must also be reconstructed. Parents have the primary responsibility in both objectives, since the school is largely responsive to their wishes. They should let the teachers and administrators know that they favor reasonable control in the classroom, even if it requires an occasional application of corporal punishment.

QUESTIONS AND ANSWERS

1. What would you do if your eighteen-year-old son decided to become a social dropout and run away to a distant city?

It is difficult for anyone to know exactly how he would face a given crisis, but I can tell you what I think would be the best reaction under those circumstances. Without nagging and whining, I would hope to influence the boy to change his mind before he made a mistake. If he could not be dissuaded, I would have to let him go. It is not wise for parents to be too demanding and authoritative with an older teen-ager; they may force him to defy their authority just to prove his independence and adulthood. Besides this, if they pound on the table, wring their hands, and scream at their wayward son, he will not feel the full responsibility for his own behavior. When mom and dad are too emotionally involved with him, he can expect them to bail him out if he runs into trouble. I think it is much wiser to treat the late adolescent like an adult; he's more likely to act like one if he is given the status offered to other adults. The appropriate parental reaction should be: "John, you know I feel you are making a choice that will haunt you for many years. I want you to sit down with me and we will analyze the pros and cons; then the final decision will be yours. I will not stand in your way." John knows that the responsibility is on his shoulders. Beginning in middle adolescence, parents should give a child more and more responsibility each year, so that when he gets beyond their control he will no longer need it.

The Gospel of St. Luke contains an amazingly relevant story of a young dropout. Let me read to you from the account in *The Living New Testament:*

"A man had two sons. When the younger told his father, 'I want my share of your estate now, instead of waiting until you die!' his father agreed to divide his wealth between his sons. A few days later this younger son packed all his belongings and took a trip to a distant land, and there wasted all his money on parties and prostitutes.

"About the time his money was gone a great famine swept over the land, and he began to starve. He persuaded a local farmer to hire him to feed his pigs. The boy became so hungry that even the pods he was feeding the swine looked good to him. And no one gave him anything. When he finally came to his senses, he said to himself, 'At home even the hired men have food enough to spare, and here I am, dying of hunger! I will go home to my father and say, "Father, I have sinned against both heaven and you, and am no longer worthy of being called your son. Please take me on as a hired man." '

"So he returned home to his father. And while he was still a long distance away, his father saw him coming, and was filled with loving pity and ran and embraced him and kissed him. His son said to him, 'Father, I have sinned against heaven and you, and am not worthy of being called your son . . .' But his father said to the slaves, 'Quick! Bring the finest robe in the house and put it on him. And a jeweled ring for his finger; and shoes! And kill the calf we have in the fattening pen. We must celebrate with a feast, for this son of mine was dead and has returned to life. He was lost and is found.' So the party began.

"Meanwhile, the older son was in the fields working; when he returned home, he heard dance music coming from the house, and he asked one of the servants what was going on. 'Your brother is back,' he was told, 'and your father has killed the calf we were fattening and has prepared a great feast to celebrate his coming home again unharmed.' The older brother was angry and wouldn't go in. His father came out and begged him. But he replied, 'All these years I've worked hard for you and never once refused to do a single thing you told me to; and in all that time you never gave me even one young goat for a feast with my friends. Yet when this son of yours comes back after spending your mon-

ey on prostitutes, you celebrate by killing the finest calf
we have on the place.' 'Look, dear son,' his father said
to him, 'you and I are very close, and everything I have
is yours. But it is right to celebrate. For he is your
brother; and he was dead and has come back to life!
He was lost and is found!' "

This story contains several important messages that are
highly relevant to our day. First, the father did not try to
locate his son and drag him home. The boy was apparently
old enough to make his own decision and the father allowed
him the privilege of determining his course. Second, the
father did not come to his rescue during the financial stress
that followed. He didn't send money. There were no well-
meaning church groups that helped support his folly. Note
in verses 16 and 17, "No one gave him anything . . . he finally came to his senses." Perhaps we sometimes keep our
children from coming to their senses by preventing them
from feeling the consequences of their own mistakes. When
a teen-ager gets a speeding citation, *he* should pay for it.
When he wrecks his car, *he* should have it fixed. When he
gets suspended from school, *he* should take the consequences
without parental protests to the school. We learn from adversity. The parent who is too anxious to bail his child out of
difficulty may be doing him a disservice. Third, the father
welcomed his son home without belittling him or demanding reparations. He didn't say, "I told you you'd make a
mess of things, big shot!" or "You've embarrassed your
mom and me to death. Everyone is talking about what a
terrible son we've raised!" Instead, he revealed the depth
of his love by saying, "He was lost and is found!"

2. Do you think the causes and the campaigns of college
   students are reasonable and legitimate? Shouldn't we
   be listening to what they are trying to tell us?

It would be simplistic to say that there is no validity or merit in the popular opinions being supported on college campuses today. I'm sure the students have some legitimate grievances which should be considered. Large, impersonal classes, for example, taught by unsophisticated graduate assistants are much too common at the undergraduate level. Students have also complained justifiably about the ridiculous "publish or perish" trend among university faculties. Very few teachers have the rare talent to stimulate, challenge, and inspire large numbers of young people; the professors who have developed this valuable skill should not be forced to spend their time conducting mediocre research in order to keep their jobs. Students are keenly aware of the professors who have outstanding teaching ability and they dread the classes of the teachers who don't — those men who are more interested in other aspects of academic life. Yet the universities continue to value something relatively unimportant to the students. There is little reward or credit given to the inspirational teachers; the universities reserve their respect and tribute for the professors who contribute to the professional literature. In this issue and in others, I believe students have a legitimate gripe against the "establishment."

Just as it is unwise to ignore everything being proclaimed by college students, it is equally foolish to adopt *all* the attitudes of the young. The over-thirty population in America is so frightened by old age that it spends a large portion of its resources trying to look, think, and act like juveniles. The individuals who are most anxious to stay young will echo any philosophy or viewpoint which identifies them with their youthful idols. This is a dangerous trend because it produces a strong political force which is largely emotional and irrational. Particularly in the area of foreign policy and politics, the under-thirty citizens lack a proper perspective of history. They do not remember the terrifying era of

Adolf Hitler. They have not lived through oppression. They have never witnessed an economic disaster. They do not understand the concept of international aggression and the consequences of appeasement.

Since the beginning of man's time on earth, ambitious tyrants have been plotting to conquer the world. There has hardly been a single period in history when someone wasn't trying to beat up everyone else. That pugnacious characteristic of human nature has not changed. There are those dictators today who are waiting for the precise moment when their claim to greatness and power can be unveiled. It is unbelieveably naïve to think that men with evil intentions have vanished from the face of the earth. How foolish is the supposition that pacifism will be honored by the Adolf Hitlers, the Mussolinis, the Atillas, the Napoleons, and the Stalins who live today! How ridiculous is the belief that freedom will go unmolested from this time forward! Yet the younger generation is not so convinced. They had not been born when a pathetic Neville Chamberlain sacrificed Europe in the name of "peace." They have not learned that strength is the only shield against the threatening ambitions of ignoble, bloodthirsty rulers. They would use the horrors of war as an excuse for surrendering to tyranny, and I pray that their opinions will change before the banner of leadership passes to them.

The question was, shouldn't we be listening to the young? Of course the students should be heard, but let's not immortalize the viewpoints of the young in the areas of their least experience.

3. How do you feel about the discipline provided by the military? Do you think the Army offers good training for a young man?

It depends on the needs of the individual. There are some

young men who badly need the kind of discipline and indoc- trination that occur in basic training. Some of these sullen, filthy, hostile young men come sauntering into the Marine Corps processing station with the same snarl and glare they used for frightening the folks back home. They stand with bent knees and stooped shoulders and mumble, "Hey, man —don't bug me, man!" Then a wiry little sergeant appears who could intimidate Dracula. He curses and ridicules them and threatens to shorten their lives; then he points to some painted feet on the pavement. Each recruit is told to put his shoes on those markers, and promised disaster if he moves even one of his little pinkies. A few hours later, these hairy adolescents are shorn absolutely bald—until nothing but ears remain amid all that skin. Then the discipline begins in earnest. They are screamed at, threatened, scoffed, and be- rated. They learn to fear and respect the authority of rank. Their individuality begins to submerge as they are molded into something they had no intention of becoming. The in- tensity of training is unbelieveably concentrated during these weeks; the recruits almost forget what it was like to ride in a car or watch television. Every waking moment (about eighteen hours a day) is spent doing something they'd rather not. When the smoke finally clears many weeks later, a man sometimes appears where a boy had been before.

Despite the positive effect this training has for some indi- viduals, the military is not an unmixed blessing. Some sen- sitive young men suffer needlessly when they are embarrassed and ridiculed. Others are already highly organized and self-disciplined before Uncle Sam reaches them. Still others find the most painful aspect of Army life to be the sheer boredom and monotony of it all. I would certainly not pre- scribe military service as a universal cure-all for the world's ills, but it is made to order for the undisciplined brat who has yet to learn respect for his superiors. Unfortunately, he is the individual who will probably be rejected by the Army for one reason or another.

4. I have observed that elementary and junior high school students — even high schoolers — tend to admire the more strict teachers. Why is this true?

Yes, the teachers who maintain order are often the most respected members of the faculties, provided they aren't mean and grouchy. A teacher who can control a class without being oppressive is almost always loved by her students. One reason is that there is safety in order. When a class is out of control, particularly at the elementary school level, the children are afraid of each other. If the teacher can't make the class behave, how can she prevent a bully from doing his thing? How can she keep the students from laughing at one of its less able members? Children are not very fair and understanding with each other, and they feel good about having a strong teacher who is.

Secondly, children love justice. When someone has violated a rule, they want immediate retribution. They admire the teacher who can enforce an equitable legal system, and they find great comfort in reasonable social rules. By contrast, the teacher who does not control her class inevitably allows crime to pay, violating something basic in the value system of children.

Thirdly, children admire strict teachers because chaos is nervewracking. Screaming and hitting and wiggling are fun for about ten minutes; then the confusion begins to get tiresome and irritating.

I have smiled in amusement many times as second and third grade children astutely evaluated the relative disciplinary skills of their teachers. They know how a class should be conducted. I only wish their teachers were equally aware of this important attribute.

5. Can you give us a guideline for how much work children should be given to do?

There should be a healthy balance between work and play. Many farm children of the past had daily chores that made life pretty difficult. Early in the morning and again after school they would feed the pigs, gather the eggs, milk the cows, and bring in the wood. Little time was reserved for fun, and childhood became a pretty drab experience. That was an extreme position and I certainly don't favor its return. However, contrast that level of responsibility with its opposite, recommended by Neill, where I shouldn't even ask my child to water the lawn or let out the cat. According to this recommendation, Junior should be allowed to lie on his overfed stomach watching six or eight hours of worthless television while his school work gathers dust in the corner. Both extremes, as usual, are harmful to the child. The logical middle ground can be found by giving the child an exposure to responsibility and work, but preserving time for his play and fun. The amount of time devoted to each activity should vary with the age of the child, gradually requiring more work as he grows older.

6. What is your opinion of the juvenile courts? Are they efficient in discouraging delinquency?

Not generally, but the blame is difficult to locate. Sometimes the courts build delinquents as systematically as if they were placing stone on stone. This happened with a ninth grader I knew who had broken every rule he could violate, just to demonstrate the toothlessness of the law. Craig would brag to his friends before committing an illegal act, and then laugh when he was not punished. In a matter of two years time he had stolen two cars, one motorcycle, run away from home twice, was suspended from school three times, and arrested once as a peeping Tom. I watched him march off to court repeatedly where he was released after receiving another worn-out lecture from the judge. Finally, Craig was sent to a camp for delinquent boys where he wrote me a letter saying how he regretted the mess he'd made of his life. He was anxious to get home and take advantage of his educational opportunity. I think Craig wanted to know how far he could push "John Law." As soon as he got the answer, he no longer wanted to fight. He should have been punished the first time he was arrested.

Shortly after hearing from Craig, I talked to a well-known judge about the obvious leniency of the courts. I asked him why juvenile authorities are so reluctant to take action against a defiant teen-ager, even though he may be begging for punishment. The judge cited two reasons for the attitudes of his colleagues: (1) There aren't enough correctional facilities available for boys like Craig. The work camps must be reserved for the greatest troublemakers. (2) It is difficult for judges to get excited about milder forms of delinquency when they have been dealing with more serious cases involving murder, rape, and robbery. It is unfortunate that the judges are limited in this fashion. A teen-ager's first encounter with the law should be so painful that he would not want to make the same mistake again, but our legal apparatus is not designed to accomplish that objective.

The juvenile courts occasionally commit the opposite error of dealing too harshly with a teen-ager. Such had been the case with Linda, a girl I met late one rainy afternoon. I was working on a report at my desk when I suddenly realized I was not alone. I looked up to see a barefoot, rain-soaked girl in my doorway. She was a pretty adolescent of about fifteen years. "You can call the police now," she instructed me.

"Why would I want to call the police?" I asked.

"Because I have run away from ...." (she named a nearby detention home for delinquent girls.) She said she'd spent the day hiding from the authorities.

She told me her name was Linda, and I asked her to sit down and tell me why she had run away. She started at the beginning and I later verified the facts to be true. Her mother had been a prostitute who gave no supervision or guidance to her daughter. Linda was even allowed to remain in the bedroom while her mother entertained her men. The child was eventually taken away from her mother and made a ward of the court. She was placed in a home for young victims where there was not enough love to go around. Her mother came to see her for the first few years, but then ignored her completely. Linda was so starved for love that she ran away to find her mother. She was immediately returned to the home. A year later she tried to escape again, with the same result. Linda continued to run away, each time becoming more sophisticated in evading the police. The year before my introduction to this girl, she had vanished again, this time being picked up by several boys. They lived together for two weeks and were involved in several misdemeanors and various sexual escapades during this period. Linda was subsequently arrested and brought before the juvenile court as a delinquent. She was sentenced to the detention center for delinquent girls, surrounded by ten-foot chain link fences. The court considered her to be an unmanageable, incorrigible adolescent, yet this was wrong. Linda was a lonely, love-starved girl who had been cheated by the circumstances of life. She needed someone to care — not someone to punish. Perhaps the judge was too busy to study her background; perhaps he had no alternative facility for Linda. Either way, the needs of this wispy girl remained unmet at this critical time of her life.

Juvenile justice must be designed to be lenient with the child who has been hurt, like Linda, and to sting the child who has challenged authority, like Craig. It is sometimes difficult to recognize the difference.

7. Aside from their drug problem and other health difficulties, the hippies seem to be having fun and enjoying themselves. Why should we force them to accept the values of our society, requiring them to worry and strain after materialistic things?

That is an excellent question and it needs to be answered. The pure theory behind hippie-dom is not such a bad idea. Our society places far too much emphasis on materialism, physical attractiveness, and status; I could sympathize with a movement to lessen the impact of these temporal values. However, what have the social dropouts selected as substitute values? The pursuit of pleasures, drug abuse, sensual gratification, sexual exploitation, sustained ignorance, filth, and venereal disease can hardly be considered improvements on the old system. All of this is done in the name of "love," which is as phony as a nine-dollar bill. Can you visualize a teen-ager offering love to a stranger on the street, but he won't even tell his worried parents where he is? That is a peculiar concept of love. It is my belief that most members of this disassociated movement have chosen their course for every possible reason other than the philosophical one. They want to be doing what others are doing, regardless of the meaning behind the behavior. If it suddenly became a symbol of "in-group" rebellion to walk on stilts and wear Mickey Mouse ears each day, we would see a mass movement in that direction. Publicity is the life blood of this herd behavior, and the communicative media are amazingly cooperative in informing the crowd of its next game. Of course, there is a minority of individuals which has chosen the hippie life through a process of rational evaluation, and they should not be discredited. Commune "families" exist which seem to have applied a new philosophy in a successful manner. However, the masses of alienated kids are marching to a set of drums called conformity.

In a more direct answer to your question, irresponsibility always offers more fun than disciplined effort. Let me ask you, who is enjoying life more, the college student who studies six hours a day to maintain a good grade average, or the carefree young rebel who spends his time rapping with his hairy friends? Certainly it is more pleasant to play than to struggle for personal achievement. But life does not end at sundown, and the future will depend on how we spend the present. "Eat, drink, and be merry, for tomorrow we die," is a dirty lie; tomorrow we *don't* die. We live to pay the bills accumulated today. I can't help but wonder what will happen to the masses of young people who are depositing the years of their youth into activities that will pay no dividends. Perhaps it is romantic to be a footloose, unemployed, independent, sensual twenty-year-old playboy, but that role is somewhat less attractive for the fat, fifty-year-old failure.

Imagine what it is like to be an aging hippie. Each morning he looks in the mirror and sees new deterioration: his face has sagged considerably, and the grooves around his eyes are branching out like streams on a map. His back hurts and his vision has blurred noticeably. What is worse, his hair has retreated to a few lonely patches around his ears, and there is *no* way he can make it symbolize rebellion. He invested his youth in nothing, and now he faces old age with no skills, no sense of worthiness, and no accomplishments to shield his ego from the cold winter storm of physical decline. Twenty years earlier he had chosen to develop temporary, unbinding relationships with all the humans in his life, so he has established no deep affection for anyone. In return, he is equally unloved. There is no one alive who remembers his youthful days. At Christmas time he takes a walk down to the local restaurant to have dinner, and as he passes the residential homes he sees families through their front windows; their fireplaces look warm and their excited children are racing back and forth in anticipation. He vaguely remembers that he chose to drop out in the name of love, but there's not much of that stuff available to him now. The most painful blow of all is delivered by the effect time has had on his social status: instead of being an advant-garde young rebel, he is now a peculiar, dirty old man. New fads and customs have replaced his archaic symbols of protest. Besides this, the new generation now views *him* with suspicion. Perhaps the only real difference between a hippie and a bum is twenty-five years. From this gloomy perspective, the best fortress against life's assaults appears to be responsibility during one's youth.

IV

The Barriers to Learning

We have been discussing the importance of discipline in the parent-child relationship, particularly as concerned with obedience, respect, and responsibility. We have also examined the importance of authority in the classroom. Now it is appropriate to examine another aspect of discipline: that dealing with the training of a child's mental faculties and moral character. The primary concern will be with the millions of children who do not succeed in school — the "academic casualties" who cannot, or will not, carry the intellectual responsibility expected of them. Their parents cry and beg and threaten; their teachers push and shove and warn. Nevertheless, they sit year after year in passive resistance to the adult coercion. Who are these youngsters for whom academic discipline seems so difficult? Are they lazy? Are they unintelligent? Do they care? Are our teaching methods ineffective? How can we help them avoid the sting of failure in these early experiences?

During my years of service as a school psychologist, I was impressed by the similarities in the students who were referred to me with learning problems. Although each child

was an individual with unique characteristics, the majority
of the youngsters shared certain kinds of problems. There
were several sets of circumstances which repeatedly inter-
fered with disciplined learning in the classroom. Described
below are those major categories of children who fail in
school; each parent is advised to look closely for the foot-
prints of his own child.

THE LATE BLOOMER

Donald is five years old and will soon go to kindergarten.
He is an immature little fellow who is still his mamma's baby
in many ways. Compared to his friends, Donald's language
is childish and his physical coordination is gross. He cries
three or four times a day, and other children take advantage of his innocence. A developmental psychologist or a
pediatrician would verify that Donald is neither physically
ill nor mentally retarded; he is merely progressing on a
slower physiological time-table than most children his age.
Nevertheless, Donald's fifth birthday has arrived, and everyone knows that middle-class five-year-olds go to kindergarten. He is looking forward to school, but deep inside he is
rather tense about this new challenge. He knows his mother
is anxious for him to do well in school, although he doesn't
really know why. His father has told him he will be a "failure" if he doesn't get a good education. He's not certain
what a failure is, but he sure doesn't want to be one. Mom
and dad are expecting something outstanding from him and
he hopes he won't disappoint them. His sister Pamela is in
the second grade now; she is doing well. She can read and
print her letters and she knows the names of every day in
the week. Donald hopes he will learn those things too.

Kindergarten proves to be tranquil for Donald. He rides the tricycle and pulls the wagon and plays with the toy clock. He prefers to play alone for long periods of time, provided his teacher, Miss Moss, is nearby. It is clear to Miss Moss that Donald is immature and unready for the first grade, and she talks to his parents about the possibility of delaying him for a year. "Flunk kindergarten? !" says his father. "How can the kid flunk kindergarten? How can anybody flunk kindergarten?" Miss Moss tries to explain that Donald has not failed kindergarten; he merely needs another year to develop before entering the first grade. The suggestion sends his father into a glandular upheaval. "The kid is six years old; he should be learning to read and write. What good is it doing him to drag around that dumb wagon and ride on a stupid tricycle? Get the kid in the first grade!" Miss Moss and her principal reluctantly comply.

The following September Donald clutches his Mickey Mouse lunch-pail and walks on wobbly legs to the first grade. From day one he begins to have academic trouble, and reading seems to be his biggest source of difficulty. His new teacher, Miss Fudge, introduces the alphabet to her class, and Donald realizes that most of his friends have already learned it. He has a little catching up to do. But too quickly Miss Fudge begins teaching something new; she wants the class to learn the sounds each letter represents, and soon he is even farther behind. Before long, the class begins to read about Dick and Jane and their immortal dog "Spot." Some children can zing right along, but Donald is still working on the alphabet. Miss Fudge divides the class into three reading groups according to their initial skill. She wants to conceal the fact that one group is doing more poorly than the others, so she gives them the camouflage names of "Lions," "Tigers," and "Giraffes." Miss Fudge's motive is noble, but she fools no one. It takes the students about two minutes to realize that the Giraffes are all stupid! Donald begins to worry about his lack of progress, and the gnawing thought looms that there may be something drastically wrong with him.

During the first parent-teacher conference in October, Miss Fudge tells Donald's parents about his problems in school. She describes his immaturity and his inability to concentrate or sit still in the classroom. "Nonsense," says his father. "What the kid needs is a little drill." He insists that Donald bring home his books, allowing father and son to sit down for an extended academic exercise. But everything Donald does irritates his father. His childish mind wanders and he forgets the things he was told five minutes before. As his father's tension mounts, Donald's productivity descends. At one point, Donald's father crashes his hand down on the table and calls his son "Stupid!" The child will never forget that knifing assessment.

Whereas Donald struggled vainly to learn during his early days in school, by November he has become disinterested and unmotivated. He looks out the window. He draws and doodles with his pencil. He whispers and plays. Since he can't read, he can neither spell, nor write, nor do his social studies. He is uninvolved and bored, not knowing what is going on most of the time. He feels fantastically inferior and inadequate. "Please stand, Donald, and read the next paragraph," says his teacher. He stands and shifts his weight from foot to foot as he struggles to identify the first word. The girls snicker and he hears one of the boys say, "What a dummy!" The problem began as a developmental lag, but has now become an emotional time-bomb and a growing hatred for school.

The tragedy is that Donald need not have suffered the humiliation of academic failure. One more year of growing and maturing would have prepared him to cope with the educational responsibilities which are now destroying him. A child's age is the *worst* possible criterion on which to determine the beginning of his school career. Six-year-old children vary tremendously in their degree of maturity; some are precocious and wise, while others are mere babies like Donald. Furthermore, the development of boys tends to be about six months behind the girls at this age. As can be seen, a slow maturing boy who turns six years old right before the beginning of school is miles behind most of his peers. This immaturity has profound social and intellectual implications.

One reason an immature child does poorly in school may be related to the absence of an organic substance called myelin. At birth, the nervous system of the body is not insulated. An infant is unable to reach out and grasp an object because the electrical command or impulse is lost on its journey from the brain to the hand. Gradually, a whitish substance (myelin) begins to coat the nerve fibers, allowing controlled muscular action to occur. Myelinization proceeds from the head downward and from the center of the body outward. In other words, a child can control the movement of his head and neck before the rest of his body. Control of the shoulder precedes the elbow, which precedes the wrist, which precedes the large muscles in the hands, which precedes small muscle coordination of the fingers. Elementary school children are taught block letter printing before they learn cursive writing because of the delayed development of minute finger control. This development pattern is of critical importance to the "late bloomer"; since visual apparatus in humans is usually the last neural mechanism to be myelinated, the immature child may not have undergone this necessary development process by the time he is six years of age. A child who is extremely immature and uncoordinated may be neurologically unprepared for the intellectual tasks of reading and writing. Reading, particularly, is a highly complex neurological process; the visual stimulus must be relayed to the brain without distortion, where it should be interpreted and retained in the memory. Not all six-year-old children are equipped to perform this task. Unfortunately, however, our culture permits few exceptions or deviations from the established timetable. A six-year-old must learn to read or he will face the emotional consequences of failure.

The question may be asked, "Why doesn't the late bloomer catch up with his class when he matures in subsequent years?" If the problem were simply a physical phenomenon, the slow maturing child could be expected to gain on his early developing friends. However, emotional factors are invariably tangled in this difficulty. The self-concept is amazingly simple to destroy but exceedingly difficult to reconstruct. Once a child begins to think of himself as stupid, incapable, ignorant, and foolish, the concept is not easily eliminated. If he is unable to function as required in the early academic setting, he is compressed in the vise-like jaws of the school and the home; the conflict is often unresolvable. There is no soothing explanation or rationalization he can offer. His personal esteem is often destroyed by this failure, and his adult personality will probably reflect the scars of a damaged ego.

The solution to the problem of the late bloomer is relatively simple: instead of scheduling the child's entrance to the first grade according to his age, the optimal timetable should be determined by neurological, psychological, social, and pediatric variables. A simple screening test could be utilized to identify the extreme cases, such as Donald. The majority of children could begin school at six years of age, although more flexibility would be reserved for the exceptional child. Regardless of the school's adoption or rejection of this recommendation, I would suggest that the parents of an immature kindergarten youngster have him examined for educational readiness by a child development expert, (child psychologist, pediatrician, neurologist, etc.) This procedure should be a "must" for slow maturing boys for whom birthdays occur late in the academic year. Our diligence in regard to this matter may spare the child a lifetime of grief.

THE SLOW LEARNER

The "slow learner" is another youngster likely to have great troubles with academic discipline, resulting from his inability to learn as quickly as his peers. I must ask the reader to endure a brief, technical explanation at this point: to understand the problem of the slow learner, we must refer to the normal distribution of intelligence quotients representing the general population.

The lightly shaded area in the center of the distribution represents the "normal range" of IQ scores, defined as those falling between 90 and 110*. Fifty percent of all individuals score within this middle area on tests of intelligence. It is interesting to note that virtually everyone thinks his IQ is above 100. If we asked 10,000 people to estimate their expected level of ability, very few would guess an IQ score below average. The fact is, half the total population would actually score below 100. Likewise, parents will often ascribe fantastic intelligence quotients to their children. A familiar but comical remark is, "Herbert has an IQ of 214, according to a test he took in the Sunday Supplement."

---

*The precise IQ points for each category will vary according to the standard deviation of the intelligence test utilized.

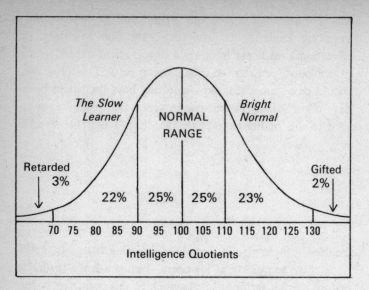

Very few individuals score above 150, and Herbert is not likely to be one of them.

The "gifted" individuals are represented at the far right of the distribution. Approximately 2 percent of all children and adults have this exceptionally bright level of ability. By contrast, nearly 3 percent of the population appears at the other end of the intellectual continuum, and are referred to as "retarded." Most states provide special education for the children with intellectual deficits, and some states offer an enriched program to the gifted.

As indicated, the purpose of presenting these statistical facts is to highlight the problems of the slow learners — those children having intelligence quotients between 70 and 90. These students comprise nearly one-fourth of the children in a typical school. In many ways, they are the saddest youngsters with whom we deal. Of particular concern are the individuals with IQs in the lower range of the slow learner classification (70 to 80) who are virtually destined to have difficulties in school. No special education is available for them, *although they are not appreciably different from the borderline retarded students.* A "retarded" child with an IQ of 70 would probably qualify for the highly specialized and expensive educational program, including a smaller class, a specially trained teacher, audio visual aids and a "no fail" policy. By contrast, a slow learning child with an IQ of 80 would usually receive no such advantages. He must compete in regular classes against the full range of students who are more capable than he. The concept of competition implies winners and losers; it is the slow learner who invariably "loses."

Let's consider the plight of the unintelligent young student in the classroom. Here is the child who "would if he could — but he can't." He will rarely, if ever, get the thrill of earning a "hundred" on his spelling test. He is the last child chosen in any academic game or contest. He often has the *least* sympathy from his teachers. He is no more successful in social activities than he is in academic pursuits, and the other children reject him openly. Like the late bloomer, the slow learner gradually develops a crushing image of failure that distorts his self-concept and damages his ego. A colleague of mine overheard two intellectually handicapped students discussing their prospects with girls; one said, "I do okay until they find out I'm a 'retard.'" Obviously, this child was keenly aware of his inferiority. What better way is there to assassinate self-confidence in our children than to place 25 percent of them in a situation where excellence is impossible to achieve, where inadequacy is the daily routine, and where inferiority is a living reality? It is not surprising that such a child often becomes a mischievous tormentor in the third grade, a bully in the sixth grade, a loudmouth in junior high, and a dropout-delinquent in high school.

The slow learner is unlike the late bloomer in one major respect: time will not resolve his deficiency. He will not do better next year. In fact, he tends to get further behind as he grows older. Traditionally, the schools have retained the incapable child in the same grade level for an extra year or two, which proves to be the most unworkable, unscientific, and unfortunate measure possible. Retention accomplishes absolutely nothing but to ice the cake of failure; the accumulated scientific evidence on this point is indisputable. Many follow-up studies have shown that children who were retained continued to fail the following year, and their academic problems were then compounded by emotional difficulties. The retained child is held back with the "little kids" while his contemporaries move on to a new grade level and a new teacher. He feels overgrown, foolish, and dumb. His relatives all know that he failed. Throughout his school career, people will ask revealing questions, such as, "How come you're thirteen years old and you're only in the fifth grade?" He will reply, "Aw, I flunked the third grade." It is a painful confession. A further problem can be anticipated: the child who is retained once or twice will undergo sexual development (puberty) one or two years before his classmates, which can produce all manner of unfortunate circumstances.

When the slow learner finally reaches high school, a year or two after he should have arrived, he usually finds even less tolerance for his difficulty. One mature tenth grader was referred to me because he announced that he was dropping out of school. I asked him why he was quitting, and he said, "I have been miserable ever since I was in the first grade. I've felt embarrassed and stupid every year. I've had to stand up and read, but I can't even understand a second grade book. You people have had your last chance to laugh at me. I'm getting out." I had to tell him I didn't blame him for the way he felt; his suffering was our responsibility.

Surprisingly, some unsuccessful students are still willing to struggle even after years of failure. It was always encouraging to see the toughest, roughest boys in high school get excited about a remedial reading program. They wanted desperately to learn this skill, but were convinced that they were too dumb. The first task of a remedial reading teacher was to show them that they *could* learn. One brawny lad named Jeff was awed by his own progress. He looked up at his teacher with tears in his eyes, and said, "When I was in the second grade I brought home a report card with an "F" in reading. I was sitting on the couch while my old man read it. He came over with a strap and beat the _____ out of me. From that time till now, this is the first time I've ever done anything right in school."

I was asked to evaluate a high school boy named Willie who had failed history three times. He was unable to graduate because he couldn't earn a "D" or better in this required course. I administered an individual intelligence test and Willie scored an IQ of 81. His teacher was surprised by this lack of ability; he had been requiring the boy to compete on an equal basis with the other students. This lack of awareness of the handicapped child seemed unfair to me, and I devised the following form letter for use in notifying teachers of slow learners like Willie.

Strictly Confidential

Name of Student _____

The above-named student apparently has some limitations which may be important to understanding his academic performance and classroom behavior. Although he does not qualify for *Special Education,* according to a strict interpretation of the Education Code, his intellectual ability seemingly falls in a "borderline" category. There is no legal basis for his removal from the regular classroom, but he should not be expected to compete with more capable students. If he is required to meet an arbitrary percentage of correct examination answers, as are students with average capabilities, he must be expected to fail consistently. On the other hand, he should not be allowed to coast along, without using the potential he has. It seems appropriate that his grade be based on the amount of effort he expends, and the learning that ensues in the light of his capacity. To fail him in spite of his efforts is to deny him the opportunity to graduate.

I would be glad to discuss the matter with you if further information is desired.

NOTE: *Please destroy this note so as to minimize the chance of causing embarrassment to the student.*

Some teachers had never considered giving a handicapped child an easier academic target until receiving this note. A few did not consider it *after* receiving this note, either.

Roberto was a pathetic, fourteen-year-old Mexican-American boy who was still in the sixth grade. He was at least five inches taller and twenty pounds heavier than the next largest student in his class. He had been retained twice, once in the second grade and again in the fourth, yet he still had not learned to read or write. His teacher sought some means of motivating the unfortunate adolescent, but Roberto had withstood all the previous gimmicks to make him work. He was simply not going to try again. The teacher finally threatened to fail him for the third time, and

Roberto responded with horror. He had heard that threat before. He could visualize himself as a seventy-three-year-old student, still sitting in a sixth grade class. He began doing his best to complete his assignments and pass the tests, but his deficient academic skills did not permit much progress. Roberto remained in a tense state of anxiety until June 16th when the final report cards were issued. On that morning, he was literally white around the mouth and shaking with tension until he read the pronouncement, "Promoted to the Seventh Grade." Roberto's teacher had not meant to be unkind; he only wanted to obtain the best effort from this lad. Nevertheless, it was a mistake to threaten him with social disaster in this manner. An unintelligent or retarded individual has the *same* emotional needs for adequacy and acceptance as a gifted or bright child, and there are some aspects of emotional stability that should not be sacrificed on the altar of education.

Despite the effects of failing a slow-learning child, I believe there are a few children who *do* profit from a second year in the same grade level. The best guideline regarding failure to promote is this: retain the child for whom something will be *different* next year. A child who was sick for seven months in one academic year might profit from another run-through when he is well. And again, the late bloomer should be held back in kindergarten (or the first grade at the latest) to place him with youngsters of comparable development. For the slow learner, however, nothing will be changed. If he was failing the fourth grade in June, he will continue to fail the fourth grade in September. It is not often realized that the curricular content of each grade level is very similar to the year before and the year after. The same concepts are taught year after year; the students in each grade are taken a little farther, but much of the time is spent in review. The arithmetical methods of addition and subtraction, for example, are taught in the primary years, but considerable work is done on these tasks in the sixth grade, too. Nouns and verbs are taught repeatedly for several years. The overlap in curricular material from grade to grade is represented more accurately by figure A, below, than by figure B.

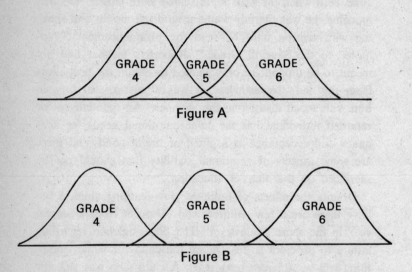

GRADE 4   GRADE 5   GRADE 6

Figure A

GRADE 4   GRADE 5   GRADE 6

Figure B

Thus, the most unjustifiable reason for retention is to give the slow learner another year of exposure to the easier concepts. He will not do better the second time around! Nor is there much magic in summer school. Some parents hope that a six-week program in July and August will accomplish what was impossible in the ten months between September and June. They are often disappointed.

Since retention and summer school do not solve the problem of the slow learner, we are faced with the obvious question: what can be done for these children? Listed below are the steps that could tip the scales in favor of this vast number of youngsters:

1. *Teach them to read, even if a one to one teacher-student ratio is required* (and it probably will be). Nearly every child can learn to read, but *many* children have difficulty if taught only in large groups. Their minds wander and they do not ask questions as readily. Certainly it would be expensive for the school to support an additional number of remedial reading teachers, but I can think of no expenditure that would be more helpful. Special techniques, teaching machines, and individual reinforcement can be successful in teaching reading — the most basic of all academic skills — to the children who are least likely to learn without individual attention. This assistance should *not* be delayed until the fourth or fifth grades or in junior high. By those late dates the child has already endured the indignities of failure.

   Many school districts have implemented creative programs to focus on reading problems. One such program, the "ungraded primary," eliminates the distinctions between students in the first three grades. Instead of grouping children by age, they are combined according to reading skill. Good readers in the first, second, and third grade may occupy the same classes. Poor readers are also grouped together. This procedure takes the sting out of retention and allows the children to profit from the benefits of homogeneous grouping. Another popular system is called the "split reading" program. In this method, the better half of the readers in a given class arrive at school thirty minutes early to be taught reading. The poorer half of the readers remain a half-hour later each evening for the same purpose. There are many such programs which have been devised to teach reading more effectively. Parents who are concerned about their child's basic academic skills may wish to seek tutorial assistance to supplement these school programs.

2. *The slow learner should be shielded from the devastation of failure.* Scholastic goals which he cannot reach should be de-emphasized. He should be required to do only the things that are within his grasp. He should be

praised when he does the best he can, even if his work isn't the same quality as his peers might produce. The "slow" child is entitled to a degree of self-acceptance too, even in this technological world.

3. *Remember that success breeds success.* The best motivation for a slow learner is to know that he is succeeding. If the adults in his life show confidence in him, he will be more likely to have confidence in himself. In fact, most humans share this same characteristic. We tend to act the way we think other people "see" us. This reality was made clear to me when I joined the National Guard. I had recently graduated from college and chose to enlist for an extended period of reserve military experience rather than to serve two years of active duty. I was immediately packed up and put on a bus for Fort Ord, California, to undergo a six-month clerical training program. Contrary to the recruiting posters, this exciting new career opportunity was not a matter of personal choice; it was selected for me. Nevertheless, the next six months were spent learning the fascinating world of military forms, typing, and filing. One hundred and eighty-three days later I returned to the local National Guard unit with this newly acquired knowledge available for usage. Surprisingly, I was not welcomed back with any overwhelming degree of enthusiasm. Everyone knows that privates are stupid. All privates are stupid. I was a private, so it stood to reason that there was thickness between my ears. With the exception of a few other stupid privates, I was out-ranked by the whole world. Everybody from the privates-first-class to the Colonel anticipated ignorant behavior from me, and to my amazement, their expectation proved accurate. The first assignment given following six months of clerical training was to type a simple letter in two copies. After investing twenty-five minutes of concentrated effort at the typewriter, I realized that the carbon paper was inserted upside down. Reverse lettering was smudged all over the back of the main copy, which did not exactly overwhelm the First Sergeant with gratitude. Similar complex procedures,

like marching "in step," were strangely difficult to perform. From today's perspective, it is clear that *my performance was consistent with my image.* Likewise, many children who fail in school are merely doing what they think others expect of them. Our reputation with our peers is a very influential force in our lives.

I have presented the problem of the slow learner — a position occupied by one-quarter of the children in today's schools. Perhaps your child is one of them.

THE UNDERACHIEVER

The underachiever is a student who is unsuccessful in school *despite* his ability to do the work. He may have an IQ of 120 or better, yet earn Ds and Fs on his report card. If possible, the underachieving children are even more numerous and less understood than the slow learners or late bloomers. The confusion is related to the fact that *two* specific ingredients are necessary to produce academic excellence, yet the second is often overlooked. First, *intellectual ability* must be there. But mental capacity is insufficient by itself. *Self-discipline* is also required. An able child may or may not have the self-control necessary to bear down day after day on something he considers painful and difficult. Intelligence and self-discipline are frequently *not* correlated. We often see a child having one without the other. Occasionally, an untalented child will struggle to achieve above his expected level; this phenomenon is termed overachievement. The opposite combination is much more common: the child with considerable intellectual potential insists upon wasting it.

It is apparent that the underachiever is handled in a way

that compounds his problem. We fail to recognize the fact that learning requires the hardest kind of effort. Examine for a moment what is required of a high school student in a daily homework assignment: he must understand what the teacher wants, including page numbers and other details; he must remember to bring home the right book; he must turn off the television set and ignore the phone in the evening; he must concentrate on the task long enough to do it correctly; he must escort the finished product safely back to class the following day; he must remember what he learned until the time of the next test. It is insufficient to complete these homework assignments once or twice; they must be done repeatedly throughout the year. This kind of performance requires something more than intelligence. The fact that a child has a good vocabulary and can put together various manipulative puzzles does not mean he can push himself week after week. Some children will succeed through the elementary school years and then give up later. In fact, it has been estimated that seventy-five percent of all students go into an academic slump sometime between the seventh and the tenth grades. Despite the frequency of this occurrence, neither the school nor the home is usually prepared to deal with it.

The typical parental reaction to the underachieving child is to select one of these three approaches: (1) Treat the problem as though it resulted from sheer stubbornness; take away the bicycle for six months, "ground" the youngster until spring, and give him the most severe blast of verbiage that can be delivered! Assuming the accuracy of my premise (that the behavior results from an understandable, childish lack of self-control) these parental reactions will certainly not make consistent bookwork any more likely to occur. Under these conditions, school takes on the blue hue of threat, which hardly makes the playboy more diligent.

Parents who become angry about underachievement in their child might also find it difficult to study if they were suddenly thrust back in school. Resistance to mental exercise is considered natural in a mature adult, but when it comes in an immature child it is assumed to reflect stubbornness. (2) The second approach is to offer the child a long-range bribe: a new bicycle in three years or a hunting trip next fall. These delayed offers are also ineffective for the reasons outlined in the previous chapter. Postponed reinforcement is tantamount to no reinforcement. (3) The third parental reaction is to say, "He's got to learn responsibility sometime! I can't always be there to help — so it's his problem."

If parents seem unrealistic in handling the difficulty, consider the school's typical reaction to underachievement. Teachers and counselors often tell the parent, "Don't worry about it. Johnny will outgrow the problem." That's their biggest falsehood of the year. Johnny usually doesn't outgrow the problem; gross underachievement in the elementary years tends to be rather permanent. Another calm message given to parents is, "Don't do anything about the problem. We'll handle it here at school," — a commitment which is rarely met.

I have dealt with more than five hundred underachievers and have come to the conclusion that there are only two functional solutions to this syndrome. The first is certainly no panacea: the parents can become so involved in the schoolwork that the child has no choice but to do the job. To make this possible, the school must expend the additional effort to communicate assignments and progress to the parents — Junior is certainly not going to carry the message! Adolescents, particularly, will confound the communication between school and home as much as possible. In one of the high schools where I served, for example, the stu-

dents had a twenty-minute "homeroom" session each day.
This time was used for the flag salute, council meetings, an-
nouncements, and related matters. Very little opportunity
for studying occurred there, yet each day hundreds of parents were told that all the homework was finished during
that session. The naïve parents were led to believe that the
homeroom period was a two-hour block of concentrated effort. Parents must know what goes on in school if they want
to program their child's academic responsibilities. They
should provide *support* in areas where pure self-discipline is
needed. The evening study period should be highly structured — routine hours and a minimum of interferences. The
parent must know what was assigned and how the finished
product should look. Finally, negative attitudes should be
withheld from the learning situation. I must hasten to say
that this procedure is not an easy solution. It rarely works
for more than a week or two, since many parents do not
have the required self-discipline themselves. There must be
a better way, and I believe there is.

The underachiever often thrives under a system of immediate reinforcement, as delineated previously. If the
child is not challenged by the rewards and motivators usually generated in the classroom, he must be fed some arti-
ficial incentives. These material rewards or other desirable
objectives should be offered, based on a definite, reachable
monetary system. Further, the reward should be applied
to small units of behavior. Instead of the reinforcement being offered to the child for earning an "A" in English at the
end of the semester, he should be given ten cents for each
properly diagrammed sentence. "Bribery!" will be the
charge from some educators. "Who cares?" is my reply, if
it puts the child to work. The use of immediate reinforcement serves the same function as a starter on a car: you
can't drive very far with it, but it gets the engine going

much easier than pushing. For the idealist who objects to the use of this extrinsic motivation, I would ask this question: "What alternative do we have, other than to 'let the child grow out of his problem'?"

Several examples may illustrate the specific application of reinforcement within the school setting. One of the most successful uses of this technique occurred with a second-grader named Billy. He had been a classic underachiever who was then enduring the second grade for the second time. His motivation had been assassinated by his early failures, and he was doing nothing in school. Furthermore, his younger sister was also in the second grade; she was promoted last year and Billy wasn't. And wouldn't you know, she was a whiz in reading, writing, and arithmetic. Billy had sunk knee-deep in intellectual despair. After a discussion with his mother, we agreed upon a motivational system to be implemented at home. On the basis of our conference, Billy's mother constructed the following chart:

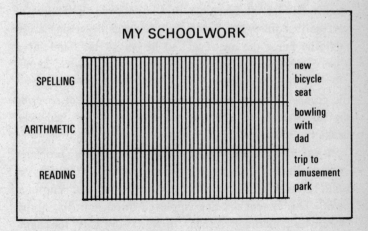

For each five minutes Billy spent working on his weekly spelling words with his mother, he received a star. When he accumulated fifty stars, he was to be given a new bicycle seat. He also received a star for each ten minutes spent working on arithmetic flash cards. Fifty stars would earn him an opportunity to go bowling with his father. Billy's mother considered reading to be his greatest problem; therefore, reading provided the pathway to a day at the amusement park (in this case, Disneyland), the biggest prize, and the stars took longer to earn (one for each fifteen minutes of reading). By staggering the reinforcement in this way, one pleasant reward was to be earned quickly, another soon after, and a grand prize waited at the end of the line. Billy caught the excitement of the game. He rushed home after school and went to work with his mother. Whereas she was previously unable to make him open a book, he suddenly wanted to "study" throughout the evening. She called me the following week to complain about not being able to get her own work done when Billy was at home. Then a strange thing began to happen. Billy began to learn, though that was not his intent. He spelled all his words correctly on the weekly test for the first time, and he enjoyed the feeling of success that followed. When the class was discussing arithmetic he knew the answers, and he waved his hand for a chance to prove his knowledge. His reading improved noticeably, and his teacher moved him out of the slow reading group. Without meaning to do so, Billy was discovering the joy of learning. The vicious cycle of failure had been broken.

It would be wrong to imply that all learning problems can be eliminated as easily and successfully as Billy's, yet reinforcement offers the best possibility of that improvement. This system is being employed throughout the world, often with remarkable results. In New York City, for example, it was realized that many of the delinquent young people were unable to read. The researchers hypothesized that the blockage in school might be related to their delinquency, and a procedure was established to work on the deficiency. The young rebels would not have responded to a direct offer to teach them to read; they had yawned through that approach too many times in school. Instead, they were told, "We have some teaching machines that may be able to teach reading; we don't know whether or not they will work. We will hire you to help us find out how successful they are. If you will work with the machines, you can earn one cent for each right answer." It was possible for the youngsters to earn $30.00 or more in the summer program. The adolescents accepted the offer and most of them learned to read, which opened new academic avenues to them. For those who were successful, delinquent behavior was no longer necessary. A similar system is being applied in the Alabama prisons, whereby inmates can earn money by learning new skills and completing instructional courses. The future will bring even wider application of these principles to difficult behavioral problems, including the one of academic underachievement.

Children and adolescents, like people of all ages, want to be responsible. They want to feel the self-respect and dignity of doing what is right. The ones who fail in school are often the most miserable, but they see no way out. The following letter is illustrative of this despair. It was written by Elaine, a very intelligent former student of mine who had seen me on a television appearance. In this unsolicited letter, she reflected the personal disgust and emptiness of irresponsible adolescence.

Dear Dr. Dobson:

I was pleasantly surprised to see you today while watching television. I was just about to change programs when you came on. Do you think they would make you a "regular" if they knew they gained a viewer by you being on?

Well, it's been four years since I talked to you. I tried once three years ago at the school carnival, but you left before I got there. Now don't you feel bad? (No!) Dr. Dobson, I'm so grateful to you for the help you gave me in school. I'm having terrible problems in school this year. I was on the verge of the emotional extreme when you knew me. Well it's worse now. I'm quite tired with the old method of teaching where the teacher trys (sic) to pound in knowledge into a captive audience that isn't even interested in a syllable she expounds. I sit in most of my classes and do absolutely nothing. I talk only when the subject interests me. I'm getting mostly Ds in most of my classes.

I ditch school quite often (like today). I average about 3 days a week at school. The only reason I go at all is because I am an active member in 4 clubs, an officer of 2 more and on the Student Council. This week has only 2 days left and I haven't been to school yet. Though I deserve it, none of my teachers will fail me. I don't do any of my assignments. They say I'm intelligent and have a lot on the ball. Ha! Ha! I ask my philosophy teacher if he thought I was a hypochondriac, [NOTE: hypochondriac is the student's name for someone who fakes illness to miss school.] He keeps boasting that he can tell in a minute, even though all of my absences are excused. Well he was right! He told me point blank that I was just dodging responsibility. Bull's eye! (No one can have malaria for two days and be bright and healthy looking the next.)

When I do go to school, I spend 1½ days a week with my counselor or any one of my teachers, talking about my problems. I avoid my real problems because I don't know what they are or I don't want to know and the people I talk to avoid telling me through our discussions what they are. They keep saying they want me to see the problems and analyze them myself. I just can't so we talk about world problems, morals, religion, etc. I may get Ds in my subjects and Fs in my work habits but I have never failed to get Os (outstanding) in my citizenship. That's one point in my favor. I'm personable and I'm not hostile.

My poor counselor is hopelessly frustrated by me. He's ready to go back to teaching (this is his first year). I know I take up a lot of his time that he could use to help someone else, like the sophomore boy who tried to commit suicide this year. But I sit in those stinken (sic) classrooms so long I think I'll scream. Anymore I just get up and walk out. My teachers, all of them, and I have come to know each other and understand each other quite well as human beings. And though they have tried, none of them have been able to help, and they realize it. So I go to my counselor and I talk and I laugh and mostly I cry.

It's almost like an obsession with me anymore to show how little I care about school, home, myself, etc. I haven't been to church for about two years, now, which doesn't mean my faith is gone. But I'm not at all dependent on it anymore. I'm very much a self-made person. How horrible that sounds because it has actually taken so many people to make me what I am (the good part of me) and a select few the bad, careless part of me.

Well, I'll bet by this time you are sorry you were on that TV show. This is a short letter compared to most that I write. I love to write down my feelings, and I get so dramatic it kills me. I could go on since you are a captive audience so to speak, but I won't. I really just wanted to drop you a line and say how happy I was to see you, and I hope the world is treating you well. I guess you are a psychologist now. I hope you never run up against someone like me.

Well on that note I will say good-bye.

Sincerely,

Elaine (...........)

P.S. I'm enclosing a picture. I don't really know why. Throw it away if you want.

Elaine has done an amazingly perceptive job of analyzing her own situation. There is meaning in every sentence. Perhaps a few comments will provide insight into the problem of other teen-agers who are floundering in the same mire.

1. Elaine is disgusted by her own folly but she lacks the self-discipline to do better. When her teacher told her she was dodging responsibility, she wrote "Bull's eye!" Now she is begging someone to help her. The long hours with her counselor are part of the search for a solution. (They also represent an easy escape from dull classes.) Even her letter to me was a lonely call for help.

2. Elaine's plea for assistance has brought sympathy but no workable answers. Her counselor would like to help, but he is a novice and lacks the needed skills. Her teachers are totally perplexed. "And though they have tried, none of them have been able to help, and they realize it. So I go to my counselor and I talk and I laugh and mostly I cry." How frustrating to have a malady for which there is no remedy. She beautifully illustrates the flaw in the modern philosophy of counseling which dictates that the counselor *listen* rather than *lead*. "I avoid my real problems . . . and the people I talk to avoid telling me through our discussions what they are. They keep saying they want me to see the problems and analyze them myself. I just can't, so we talk about world problems, religion, etc." As a blind man might need direction, Elaine needs someone to take her by the hand and lead her out of the darkness.

3. Elaine's truancy is an attempt to dramatize her predicament. It is part of her "obsession to show how little she cares about school, home, myself, etc." If she can make known her need, perhaps someone will come to her rescue. Furthermore, she wants to make it clear that her failure is occurring because she hasn't tried, rather than because of an inability to succeed.

4. Elaine's *basic* problem emanates from a great lack of self-respect. The comment about my destroying her picture reflected her dissatisfaction with her physical appearance. She is considerably overweight — a symptom of the same lack of self-control. Additional aspects of her personal devaluation appeared in other parts of the letter. I think she was so busy dealing with this low esteem that academic work was impossible.
5. Elaine did not want to fight with anybody. She was not defiantly challenging the system. She was merely calling for assistance. As she put it, "I am personable and not hostile."

Elaine's problem was deeply ingrained and rigid; her long-standing attitudes could not be eradicated by glib "solutions." She needed extended counseling from a wise and understanding adult who could lead her step by step into a position of more responsible behavior. One thing is certain: virtually everything being done at school was harmful. Elaine was not being aided by the permissive attitude of the school toward her truancy. Her teachers were not exercising wisdom by allowing her to roam in and out of class. They were not helping Elaine by giving her Ds instead of Fs, despite her admission that she neither came to class nor completed any of her assignments. She knew she deserved to fail. Her counselor was not teaching self-control by letting her rattle on hour after hour about "world problems" whenever she chose to walk out of class. Certainly, Elaine did not need criticism and reproof, but neither did she profit from the school's cooperation in her folly. Parents may also be guilty of fostering irresponsibility in the name of "understanding."

Underachievers, like Elaine and Billy, are too numerous to be ignored in the nation's schools. When combined with the slow learners and late bloomers, they constitute a considerable portion of the school population. These young failures need patient and careful instruction in developing the skills of self-discipline which have somehow escaped them.

SUMMARY

I have described three great sources of interference with discipline in the classroom. Certainly, there are additional problems which I have not presented in detail. Anything that worries or troubles a child can result in school failure. For example, deep feelings of inadequacy and inferiority can prevent concentration on academic endeavors; the child who is busy coping with such overwhelming emotions has little time for less important matters. The adult who has ever tried to work or think while awaiting a threatening medical report, such as a laboratory evaluation for cancer, may understand this mechanism of mental interference.

Parents and teachers must never underestimate the threats a child associates with school. Regardless of whether or not he verbalizes his fears, he is often aware of many "dangers" which lurk behind the hallowed walls of Abraham Lincoln Junior High. Other students might laugh at him. He may be ridiculed or criticized by his teachers. He could be rejected by members of the opposite sex. He may fail despite his best efforts. These and similar fears can permeate the entire world of a bewildered young student, causing him to act in a way which makes him appear lazy. Thus, the solution to school failure often requires the elimination of problems which seem unrelated to classroom work.

QUESTIONS AND ANSWERS

1. If age is such a poor factor to use in determining the

start of the first grade, why is it applied so universally in our country?

Because it is so convenient. Parents can plan for the definite beginning of school when their child reaches six years of age. School officials can survey their districts and know how many first-graders they will have the following year. If an eight-year-old moves into the district in October, the administrator knows with certainty that the child belongs to the second grade, and so on. The use of chronological age as a criterion for school entrance is great for everybody — except the late bloomer.

2. What causes a child to be a slow learner?

There are many hereditary, environmental, and physical factors which contribute to one's intellect, and it is difficult to isolate the particular influences. However, accumulating evidence seems to indicate that dull normal intelligence and even borderline retardation are often caused by a lack of intellectual stimulation in the child's very early years. There appears to be a critical period during the first three to four years when the potential for intellectual growth must be seized. If the opportunity is missed, the child may never reach the capacity which had originally been available to him. The dull child is often one who has not heard adult language regularly; he has not been provided with interesting books and puzzles to occupy his sensory apparatus; he has not been taken to the zoo, the airport, or other exciting places; he has grown up with a minimum of daily training and guidance from adults. The lack of stimulation available to such a child may result in the failure of his brain to develop properly.

The effect of early stimulation on living brains was studied in several fascinating animal experiments conducted by an investigator named Kretch. He and his associates divided litter-mate rats into two identical groups; one group was destined to receive maximum stimulation during the first few months of life. The rats were kept in well-lighted cages, surrounded by interesting paddle wheels and other toys. They were handled regularly and allowed to explore outside their cages. They were subjected to learning experiences and then rewarded for remembering. The second group of rats lived the opposite kind of existence. They crouched in dimly lit, drab, uninteresting cages. They were not handled or stimulated in any way, and were not permitted outside their cages. Both groups were fed identical food. At 105 days of age, all the rats were sacrificed to permit examination of their neurological apparatus. The researchers were surprised to find that the high stimulation rats had brains that differed in several important ways: (1) The cortex (the thinking part of the brain) was thicker and wider; (2) The blood supply was much more abundant; (3) the enzymes necessary for learning were more sophisticated. The researchers concluded that high stimulation experienced during the rats' early lives had resulted in more advanced and complex brains.

It is always risky to apply the conclusions of animal research directly to humans, but the same kinds of changes probably occur in the brains of highly stimulated children. If parents want their children to be capable, they should begin by talking to them at length while they are still babies. Interesting mobiles and winking-blinking toys should be arranged around the crib. From then on through the toddler years, learning activities should be programmed regularly. Of course, parents must understand the difference between stimulation and pressure. Providing books for a three-year-old is stimulating; ridiculing and threatening him because he can't read them is pressuring. Imposing unreachable expectations can have a damaging effect on children.

If early stimulation is as important as it now appears, then poverty and ghetto life may be the leading cause of mental sluggishness and mild retardation. This may explain why the children of minority groups score lower on IQ tests than members of higher socio-economic groups; their parents have neither the time nor the resources to invest in them. The necessity for providing rich, edifying experiences for young children has never been so obvious as it is today.

3. I've read that it is possible to teach three-year-old children to read. Should I be working on this with my child?

If a youngster is particularly sharp and if he can learn to read without feeling undue adult pressure, it might be advantageous to teach him this skill. Those are big "if's," though. Few parents can work with their own children without showing frustration over natural failures. It's like teaching your wife to drive: risky, at best — disastrous at worst. Besides this limitation, learning should be programmed at the age when it is most needed. Why invest unending effort in teaching a child to read when he has not yet learned to cross the street, or tie his shoes, or count to ten, or answer the telephone? It seems foolish to get panicky over preschool reading, as such. The best policy is to provide your children with many interesting books and materials, read to them and answer their questions, then let nature take its unobstructed course.

4. Should school children be required to wear "cute" clothes which they dislike?

Generally not. Children are very concerned about the threat of being laughed at by their friends, and they will sometimes go to great lengths to avoid that possibility. The major push behind their desire to conform is the fear of ridicule. Teen-agers, particularly, seem to feel, "The group can't laugh at me if I am identical to them." From this perspective, it is unwise to make a child endure unnecessary social humiliation. Children should be allowed to select their own clothes, within certain limits of the budget and of good taste.

5. Some educators have said we should eliminate report cards and academic marks. Do you think this is a good idea?

No, academic marks are valuable for students in the third grade or higher. They serve as a form of reinforcement — as a reward for the child who has achieved in school and as a nudge to the youngster who hasn't. It is important, though, that marks be used properly; they have the power to create or to destroy motivation. Through the elementary years and in the required courses of high school, a child's grades should be based on what he does with what he has. In other words, we should grade according to ability. A slow child should be able to succeed in school just as certainly as a gifted youngster. If he struggles and sweats to achieve, he should be rewarded with a symbol of accomplishment even if his work falls short of an absolute standard. By the same token, the gifted child should not be given an "A" just because he is smart enough to excel without working.

Our primary purpose in grading should be to reward academic effort. For those individuals who disagree with this grading policy, they should consider the alternative reflected in the following illustration: Slow Joe is something less than brilliant and he knows it. He has never done well in school and he quit trying when he was in the second grade. However, when he reached the sixth grade he was taught by a man who challenged him to do his best. He worked very hard to please this teacher, despite his problems with reading, writing, and arithmetic. At the end of the term, Slow Joe was still hard at work, although his writing had improved little and he was struggling with a third grade reader. What was his teacher to do with Slow Joe's report card? If he graded the youngster in relation to his peers, he would have to fail him. If he failed him, Joe would never work again. Joe had done his best — should he then be given the same grade he got last year when he sat blunk-eyed day after day? I think not. Joe should be praised for his diligence in the most obvious manner, and given at least Cs, if not higher, on his report card. His parents should be informed of his more realistic performance, and their support should be enlisted in encouraging Joe's continued effort. Any other system of grading will result in discouragement to children of lesser ability. Even the sharper students usually work better when they must stretch to reach a position of excellence.

One exception to the "grade on ability" policy should be implemented: college preparation courses in high school must be graded on an absolute standard. An "A" in chemistry or Latin is accepted by college admission boards as a symbol of excellence, and high school teachers must preserve that meaning. But then, Slow Joe and his friends need not be in those difficult courses.

To repeat, marks can be the teacher's most important motivational tool — provided they are used correctly. Therefore, the recommendation that schools eliminate grading is a move away from discipline in the classroom.

6. It is my understanding that we forget eighty percent of everything we learn in three months' time and a higher percentage is forgotten as time passes. Why, then, should we put children through the agony of learning? Why is mental exercise needed if the effort is so inefficient?

Your question reflects the viewpoint of the old progressive education theorists. They wanted the school curriculum to be nothing more than "life adjustment." They placed a low priority on intellectual discipline for the reasons you mentioned. Even some college professors have adopted this "no content" philosophy; they reason that the material we learn today may be obsolete tomorrow, so why learn it? I strongly disagree with this approach to education. There are at least five reasons why learning is important, even if a high incidence of forgetting does take place: (1) Perhaps the most important function of school, apart from teaching the basic literary and mathematical skills, is to foster self-discipline and self-control. The good student learns to sit for long hours, follow directions, carry out assignments and channel his mental faculties. Homework, itself, is relatively unnecessary as an educational tool, but it is valuable as an instrument of discipline. Since adult life often requires self-sacrifice, sweat, and devotion to causes, the school should play a role in shaping a child's capacity to handle this future responsibility. Certainly, play is important in a child's life too. He should not work all the time; the home and school should provide a healthy balance between discipline and play. (2) Learning is important because we are *changed* by what we learn, even if the facts are later forgotten. No college graduate could remember everything he learned in school, yet he is a very different person for having gone to college. Learning produces alterations in values, attitudes, and concepts which do not fade in time. (3) Even if the learned material cannot be recalled, the individual knows the facts exist and where he can find them. If we asked a complicated question of an uneducated man, he would be likely to give a definite, unqualified response. The same question would probably be answered more cautiously by a man with a doctor's degree; he would say, "Well, there are several ways to look at it." He knows the matter is more complex than it appears, even if he doesn't have the full answer. (4) We don't forget one hundred percent of what we learn. The most important facts take their place in our permanent memory for future use. The human brain is capable of storing two billion bits of data in a lifetime; education is the process of filling that memory bank with useful information. (5) Old learning makes new learning easier. Each mental exercise gives us more associative cues with which to link future ideas and concepts.

I wish there were an easier, more efficient process for shaping human minds than the slow, painful experience of education. I'm afraid we'll have to depend on this old-fashioned approach until a "learning pill" is developed.

V

Discipline in Morality

In 1968, a motion picture producer appearing on nation-wide television made the startling prediction that the photography of sexual intercourse would be permissible in movies by 1978. His statement was thought by many to be a deliberate exaggeration — "could they ever go that far?" The producer missed his estimate by nine years; less than twelve months after the comment was made, his prediction became a reality in numerous motion pictures. This rapid reversal of sexual mores is unparalleled in man's history. Never has a society abandoned its concept of morality more suddenly than occurred in America during the decade of the sixties.

Although the basic ethical structure came crashing down during this brief period, the erosion of traditional morality began much earlier. The change was engineered by several key forces — each having a financial motive. Shortly after World War I, the entertainment industry discovered that considerable profit could be made by the exploitation of sex and daring new attitudes. Advertisement executives on Madison Avenue soon learned the same lesson, as did publishers and other manipulators of social opinion. Through the years they subtly undercut the importance of sexual morality, honesty, personal integrity, and meaningful faith in God. By the beginning of the sixties, Americans were wondering whether it was really so necessary to inhibit their sensual passions and impulses. "Fun and games" looked marvelous, and after all, life was meant to be enjoyed. At this precise moment of social questioning, the Playboy Philosophy appeared with its redefinition of immorality; sexual irresponsibility suddenly became dignified and as pure as the driven snow. Believers in traditional morality were depicted as finger-wagging old hypocrites who were probably concealing a little hanky-panky of their own. After the development of penicillin (to prevent disease) and the Pill (to prevent babies), only one nagging thought inhibited widespread acceptance of the new attitude: how did God view this sexual innovation? Long ago He had threatened "Thou shalt not!" in terms that were difficult to misinterpret. This final barrier was conveniently eliminated by the theologians themselves, who announced their amazing conclusion in 1966 that "God is dead!" The way was paved for a sweeping sexual revolution which has still not reached its peak.

Not everyone in our society has allowed passion to overrule judgment. There are those who still believe, as I do, that sexual irresponsibility carries an enormous price tag for the momentary pleasure it promises. Despite the reassuring philosophy of Hugh Heffner and his Playmates, sexual "freedom" is a direct thoroughfare to disillusionment, emptiness, divorce, venereal disease, illegitimacy, and broken lives. Not only do promiscuous individuals suffer adverse consequences; history reveals that entire societies begin to deteriorate when free love reaches a position of social acceptance. This fact was first illuminated by J. D. Unwin, a British social anthropologist who spent seven years studying the births and deaths of eighty civilizations. He reported from his exhaustive research that every known culture in the world's history has followed the same sexual pattern: during its early days of existence, premarital and extramarital sexual relationships were strictly prohibited. Great creative energy was associated with this inhibition of sexual expression, causing the culture to prosper. Much later in the life of the society, its people began to rebel against the strict prohibitions, demanding the freedom to release their internal passions. As the mores weakened, the social energy abated, eventually resulting in the decay or destruction of the civilization. Dr. Unwin stated that the energy which holds a society together is sexual in nature. When a man is devoted to one woman and one family, he is motivated to build, save, protect, plan, and prosper on their behalf. However, when his sexual interests are dispersed and generalized, his effort is invested in the gratification of sensual desires. Dr. Unwin concluded: "Any human society is free either to display great energy, or to enjoy sexual freedom; the evidence is that they cannot do both for more than one generation." America is not likely to be the first to succeed in fulfilling these opposing purposes.

I have devoted the remainder of this chapter to the parents and teachers who believe in moral decency and want to instill responsible sexual attitudes in their children. Their task is not an easy one. The sexual urge is stronger during adolescence than in any other period of life, and there is no way to guarantee that an independent teen-ager will choose to control it. It is impossible, and probably undesirable, to shield him from the permissive attitudes which are prevalent today; television brings every element of the sexual revolution into the sanctuary of one's living room, and the details of immorality and perversion are readily available in the theater or from the neighborhood smut dealer. Obviously, solitary confinement of the child is not the answer. Furthermore, there is a danger that parents will make one mistake in their efforts to avoid another. While attempting to teach discipline in matters of morality, they must be careful not to inculcate unhealthy attitudes that will interfere with sexual fulfillment in future marital relations. Those who would teach this subject have the difficult responsibility of saying "sex can be wonderful" and "sex can be dangerous" in the same breath, which takes some doing. How then can conscientious adults instill self-control in their children without generating deep emotional hangups or negative attitudes? Discussed below are the aspects of sex education which are critical to the achievement of this delicate balance.

WHO SHOULD TEACH THE CHILD ABOUT SEX?

The task of forming healthy sexual attitudes and understandings in children requires considerable skill and tact, and parents are often keenly aware of their lack of preparation for this assignment. However, for those parents who *are* able to handle the instructional process correctly, the responsibility should be retained in the home. There is a growing trend for all aspects of education to be taken from the hands of parents (or the role is deliberately forfeited by them). This is a mistake. Particularly in the matter of sex education, the best approach is one that begins in early childhood and extends through the years, according to a policy of openness, frankness, and honesty. Only parents can provide this lifetime training. The child's needs for information and guidance are rarely met in one massive conversation which is typically provided by reluctant parents as their child approaches adolescence. Nor does a concentrated formal educational program outside the home offer the same advantages provided by a gradual enlightenment that begins during the third or fourth year of life and reaches a culmination shortly before puberty.

Despite the desirability of sex education's being handled by highly skilled parents, one must admit that this is an idealistic objective in many homes (perhaps the majority of them). Parents are often too sexually inhibited to present the subject with poise, or they may lack the necessary technical knowledge of the human body. For such families which cannot, or will not, teach their children the details of human reproduction, there must be outside agencies that will assist them in this important function. Whether or not that service should be provided by the schools or some other institution depends on what will be taught in the particular program.

The issue of what to teach in formal sex education classes is of great importance to the parents who resist society's liberalized attitudes toward sex. For the children of Christian families or others with firm convictions about moral behavior, an acceptable sex education program must consist of two elements. First, the physiology of reproduction should be taught. Basic anatomy of the human body should be presented as well as the mechanics of sexual behavior in marriage. In other words, the technology of sex represents the primary content on which to focus. However, this first objective represents only half of the task. The second critical element involves the obligation to teach moral attitudes and the responsibilities related to sex. *These components should never be separated as long as the issue of morality is considered important!* Sexual sophistication without sexual responsibility is sexual disaster! To explain all the mechanics of reproduction without teaching the proper attitudes and controls is like giving a child a loaded gun without

showing him how to use it. Nevertheless, this second responsibility is often omitted or minimized in the public school
setting. The Supreme Court decision prohibiting prayer in
schools caused teachers and administrators to be extremely
self-conscious about any subject having religious overtones.
They have been required to meet the least common denom-
inator on spiritual or moral matters, meaning the subject is
usually avoided altogether. Even if the ethical considera-
tions are introduced in the classroom, they may be presented
according to the concept of moral relativism. This philosophy is nothing more than a sneaky endorsement of gross
immorality. According to the precepts of moral relativism,
premarital sexual experiences are proper if the participants
have a "meaningful relationship" going for them. Isn't that
sweet? A couple can purify their sexual relationship if they
can convince themselves that they like each other. Adolescents mature sexually at least four or five years before they
reach emotional maturity. Thus, most fifteen-year-olds
wouldn't know a "meaningful relationship" if they faced one
in broad daylight. They lose all objectivity when influenced
by a full moon — or a strong rock beat — or a well en-
dowed partner. They're madly in love for at least twelve
hours. Could there be any more flimsy matter on which to
base an important decision than an adolescent's interpretation of love? From this viewpoint, moral relativism appears
worse than a blatant recommendation of sexual promiscuity because it lends an atmosphere of pseudomorality to the
behavior.

Despite their wish to avoid the issue of morality, sex education teachers find it almost impossible to remain neutral
on the subject. Students will not allow them to conceal their
viewpoint. "But what do you think about premarital intercourse, Mr. Burgess?" If Mr. Burgess refuses to answer this
question, he has inadvertently told the students that there

is no definite right or wrong involved. By not taking a stand for morality he has endorsed promiscuity. The issue appears arbitrary to his students, rendering it more likely that their intense biological desires will get satisfied.

I would like to stress the fact that I am not opposed to sex education in the public schools — provided both elements of the subject are presented properly. Simply stated, I don't want my children taught sex technology by a teacher who is either neutral or misinformed about the consequences of immorality. It would be preferable that Junior would learn his concepts in the streets than for a teacher to stand before his class, having all the dignity and authority invested in him by the school and society, and tell his impressionable students that traditional morality is either unnecessary or unhealthy. Unless the schools are prepared to take a definite position in favor of sexual responsibility (and perhaps the social climate prevents their doing so), some other agency should assist concerned parents in the provision of sex education for their children. The churches could easily provide this service for society. The YMCA, YWCA, or other social institutions might also be helpful at this point. Perhaps there is no objective that is more important to the future of our nation than the teaching of moral discipline to the most recent generation of Americans.

Let's turn our attention to other principles of sex education which parents should consider in fulfilling their important responsibility.

WHEN TO SAY WHAT

Even in this enlightened day, the subject of sex is charged with emotion. There are few thoughts which disturb Mom and Dad's tranquillity more than the vision of answering all of Junior's probing questions — particularly the ones which will get uncomfortably personal. This parental tension was apparent in the mother of nine-year-old Davie, after his family had recently moved into a new school district. Davie came home from school on the first afternoon and asked his mother point-blank: "Mom, what's sex?" The question smacked her hard; she thought she had two or three years before dealing with that issue and she was totally unprepared to field it now. Her racing mind concluded that Davie's new school must be engaged in a liberal sex education program that had introduced the subject to him, and she had no choice but to fill in the details. She sat down with her wide-eyed son, and for forty-five minutes of sheer tension she gave him a dry-mouthed, sweaty-palmed harangue about the birds and the bees and the coconut trees. When she finally finished, Davie held up his enrollment card and said, "Gee, Mom, how am I going to get all that in this little bitty square?" As Davie's mother discovered, there is a delicate art in knowing when to provide the younger generation with additional information about sex.

One of the most common mistakes committed by some parents and many overzealous educators is the trend toward teaching too-much-too-soon. In some school districts, for example, kindergarten children are shown films of animals in the act of copulation. There is no apparent gain to be harvested from plunging headlong into sex education in this fashion. In fact, available evidence indicates that there are numerous hazards involved in moving too rapidly. A child can sustain a severe emotional jolt by being exposed to realities for which he is not prepared. Furthermore, it is unwise to place the youngster on an informational timetable that will result in full sophistication too early in life. If an eight-year-old boy is given an advanced understanding of mature sexual behavior, it is less likely that he will wait ten or twelve years to apply his knowledge within the confines of marriage. Another danger resulting from premature instruction involves the threat of overstimulation. A child can be tantalized by what he is taught about the exciting world of grown-up sexual experience. Childhood should be devoted to childish interests — not adult pleasures and desires. I am not implying that sex education should be delayed until childhood has passed. Rather, it seems appropriate that the amount of information a youngster is given should coincide with his social and physical requirement for that awareness.

The child's requests for information provide the best guide to his readiness for sex education. His comments reveal what he is thinking about and the facts he wants to know. His questions also offer a natural vehicle for instruction. It is far better for his parents to answer these questions at the moment of curiosity than to ignore or evade them, hoping to explain later. Premeditated training sessions often become lengthy, one-way conversations which make both participants uncomfortable. Although the question-answering approach to sex education is usually superior, the technique is obviously inadequate for use with children who never ask for information. Some boys and girls are fascinated by sexual reproduction while others never give it a second thought. If a child is uninterested in the subject of sex, the parent is not relieved of his responsibility by the absence of questions. The use of small animals, as described in the following section, is an excellent way to generate the necessary curiosity.

One final comment is important regarding the timing of sex education in the home. Parents should plan to end their instructional program immediately before their child enters puberty (the time of rapid sexual development in early

adolescence). Puberty usually begins between ten and seventeen years of age for girls and between twelve and nine-
teen for boys. Once they enter this developmental period,
they are typically embarrassed by discussions of sex with
their parents. Adolescents usually resent adult intrusion
during this time, preferring to have the subject of sex ignored in the home. We should respect their wish. We are
given ten or twelve years to provide the proper understanding of human sexuality; after that foundation has been constructed, we can only serve as resources to whom the child
can turn if he chooses.

ASSISTANCE FROM MOTHER NATURE

As indicated above, small animals can be very helpful in
the process of sex education. I can think of no better audio-visual aid than a pregnant cat who is not sensitive about
being observed. The subject of reproduction can be grace-
fully presented after an animal has demonstrated the process of birth. I heard of a seven-year-old boy who left his
mother this note: "Dear Mom. Our poor kitty came all apart
in the garidge today. Love, Richard." Mom rushed out to
the "garidge" to find that the cat had given birth to six little
kittens. She and Richard held an important conversation
that evening about kitties and babies and such things. This
natural introduction to sexual reproduction was inevitable
for children raised on farms, but city children often experience nothing more helpful than an abstract explanation. I
would recommend that parents get their children a prolific
pet. If Dad just can't stand cats, then dogs, hamsters, or
any other mammals can be of assistance.

SEX AND THE ADOLESCENT

It is important for parents to understand the physical and emotional characteristics of puberty. First, the glandular and hormonal influences result in rapid sexual development of the body. This accelerated maturation generates a greatly increased interest in the opposite sex. During the early days of puberty, it is common for a teen-ager to concentrate on sex most of the time. He is fascinated by this exciting new world and he wants to learn all he can about it. A word of advice might be timely at this point: parents should not be shocked by what they see or hear from a pubescent child; he is liable to say or write nearly anything. The most timid little monosyllabic adolescent can sometimes compose the most astonishing profanity. This kind of sexual exploration should not be considered indicative of moral decay — it typically signals the child's sudden fascination with sex. Along with the newly acquired interest in sex comes a considerable amount of anxiety and concern. The threat emanates from many related sources. A tense adolescent may repeatedly ask himself scores of questions concerning his sexual development: "Are all these changes supposed to be happening? Is there something wrong with me? Do I have a disease or an abnormality? Does this pain in my breasts mean I have cancer? Will I be sexually adequate? Will the boys laugh at me? Will the girls reject me? Will God punish me for the sexual thoughts I have? Wouldn't it be awful if I became a homosexual? Could I get pregnant without having sexual relations? Do some people fail to mature sexually? Could I be one of those people? Will my modesty be sacrificed?" These kinds of fears are almost universal among early adolescents. In fact, it is almost impossible to grow up in our culture without some worry and concern about sexuality. This tension is often carried over

into adult marital life. Under the proper atmosphere of acceptance, a church or other agency can provide a setting to
elicit these questions and allay the fears during the period
of greatest concern.

CONCLUSION

In a day of sudden sexual revolution, parental attempts
to teach basic morality to their children become extremely
difficult. The discipline of adolescent sexual drives has never been easy, even when society was supportive of its importance. But our culture now agitates against traditional
morality. Our youngsters are immersed in a world which
is questioning the value of premarital virginity; even marital
fidelity is less important than it was a few years ago. The
message of sexual freedom is being preached with evan-
gelistic fervor in the theater, television, magazines, radio,
and in the recording industry. Sex is used to sell everything from toothpaste to breakfast cereal. A motel mar-
quee suggests to its patrons: "Have your next affair with us."
A magazine advertisement for a feminine hygiene product
pictures a nude girl who says, "Relax and enjoy the revolution!" Children and adolescents are not deaf to these
voices. Their society is overwhelmingly preoccupied with
sex and their parents cannot divorce them from its influence. How can concerned families counterbalance these
forces which surround their impressionable children and
how can they instill positive attitudes toward the healthy
meaning of sex?

In the first chapter of this book I discussed the importance
of the child's respect for his parents. His attitude toward
their leadership is critical to his acceptance of their values

and philosophy, including their concept of premarital sexual behavior. Likewise, the most fundamental element in teaching morality can be achieved through a healthy parent-child relationship during the early years. The obvious hope is that the adolescent will respect and appreciate his parents enough to believe what they say and accept what they recommend. Unfortunately, however, this loyalty to parents is often an insufficient source of motivation. It is my firm conviction that children should also be taught ultimate loyalty to God. We should make it clear that the merciful God of love whom we serve is also a God of wrath. If we choose to defy His moral laws we will suffer certain consequences. God's spiritual laws are as inflexible as His physical laws. If a man jumps from the top of a twenty-story building he will die as his body crashes to the earth below; likewise, the willful violation of God's commandments is equally disastrous, for "the wages of sin is death." An adolescent who understands this truth is more likely to live a moral life in the midst of an immoral society.

One further comment may be relevant. I hope to give my daughter a small, gold key on her tenth birthday. It will be attached to a chain to be worn around her neck, and will represent the key to her heart. Perhaps she will give that key to one man only — the one who will share her love through the remainder of her life.

QUESTIONS AND ANSWERS

1. Should a child be allowed to "decide for himself" on matters related to his concept of God? Aren't we forcing our religion down his throat when we tell him what he must believe?

Let me answer that question with an illustration from nature. A little gosling (baby goose) has a peculiar characteristic that is relevant at this point. Shortly after he hatches from his shell he will become attached, or "imprinted," to the first thing that he sees moving near him. From that time forward, he will follow that particular object when it moves in his vicinity. Ordinarily, he becomes imprinted to the mother goose who was on hand to hatch the new generation. If she is removed, however, the gosling will settle for any mobile substitute, whether alive or not. In fact, a gosling will become imprinted most easily to a blue football bladder, dragged by on a string. A week later, he'll fall in line behind the bladder as it scoots by him. Time is the critical factor in this process. The gosling is vulnerable to imprinting for only a few seconds after he hatches from the shell; if that opportunity is lost, it cannot be regained later. In other words, there is a critical, brief period in the life of the gosling when this instinctual learning is possible.

There is also a critical period when certain kinds of instruction are possible in the life of the child. Although humans have no instincts (only drives, reflexes, urges, etc.), there is a brief period during childhood when youngsters are vulnerable to religious training. Their concepts of right and wrong, which Freud called the superego, are formulated during this time, and their view of God begins to solidify. As in the case of the gosling, the opportunity of that period must be seized when it is available. Leaders of the Catholic Church have been widely quoted as saying, "Give us a child until he is seven years old and we'll have him for life"; their affirmation is usually correct, because permanent attitudes can be instilled during these seven vulnerable years. Unfortunately, however, the opposite is also true. The absence or misapplication of instruction through that prime-time period may place a severe limitation on the depth of the child's later devotion to God. When parents say they are going to withhold indoctrination from their small child, allowing him to "decide for himself," they are almost guaranteeing that he will "decide" in the negative. If a parent wants his child to have a meaningful faith, he must give up any misguided attempts at objectivity. The child listens closely to discover just how much his parent believes what he is preaching; any indecision or ethical confusion from the parent is likely to be magnified in the child.

After the middle adolescent age, (thirteen to fifteen years,) a child resents being told exactly what to believe; he does not want religion "forced down his throat," and should be given more and more autonomy in what he believes. If the early exposure has been properly conducted, he will have an inner mainstay to steady him. That early indoctrination, then, is the key to the spiritual attitudes he will carry into adulthood.

2. My daughter recently told me that she is two months pregnant. What should be my attitude to her now?

You cannot reverse the circumstances by being harsh or unloving at this point. Your daughter needs more understanding now than ever before, and you should give it to her if possible. Help her grope through this difficulty and avoid "I told you so" comments. Many important decisions will face her in the next few months and she will need a cool, rational mother to assist in determining the best path to take. Remember that lasting love and affection often develop between people who have survived a crisis together.

3. When do children begin to develop a sexual nature? Does this occur suddenly during puberty?

No, it occurs long before puberty. Perhaps the most important scientific fact suggested by Freud was his observation that children are not asexual. He stated that sexual gratification begins in the cradle and is first associated with feeding. Behavior during childhood is influenced considerably by sexual curiosity and interest, although the happy hormones do not take full charge until early adolescence. It is not uncommon for a four-year-old to be fascinated by nudity and the sexual apparatus of boys versus girls. This is an important time in the forming of sexual attitudes; parents should be careful not to express shock and extreme disapproval of this kind of curiosity. It is believed that many sexual problems begin as a result of inappropriate training during early childhood.

4. Many American colleges and universities are permitting men and women to live in coeducational dormitories, often rooming side by side. Others now allow unrestricted visiting hours by members of the opposite sex. Do you think this promotes more healthy attitudes toward sex?

It certainly promotes more sex, and some people think that's healthy. The advocates of cohabitation try to tell us that young men and women can live together without doing what comes naturally. That is nonsense. The sex drive is one of the strongest forces in human nature, and Joe College is notoriously weak in suppressing it. I would prefer that the supporters of coeducational dormitories admit that morality is not very important to them. If morality is something we value, then we should at least give it a wobbly-legged chance to survive. The sharing of collegiate bedrooms hardly takes us in that direction.

5. Do you think religion should be taught in the public schools?

Not as a particular doctrine or dogma. The right of parents to select their child's religious orientation must be protected and no teacher or administrator should be allowed to contradict what he has been taught at home. On the other hand, the vast majority of Americans do profess a belief in God. I would like to see this unnamed God acknowledged in the classroom. The Supreme Court decision banning nonspecific school prayer (or even silent prayer) is an extreme measure, and I regret it. The tiny minority of children from atheistic homes could be easily protected by the school during prayful moments.

6. My teen-age daughter has admitted having sexual relations with several boys. Since she doesn't believe in God she sees no reason for doing otherwise. What can I tell her?

You might make her aware of the fact that sexual freedom is expensive and most of the bills are paid by women. The natural sex appeal of girls serves as their primary source of bargaining power in the game of life. In exchange for feminine affection and love, a man accepts a girl as his lifetime responsibility — supplying her needs and caring for her welfare. This sexual aspect of the marital agreement can hardly be denied. Therefore, a girl who indiscriminately gives away her basis for exchange has little left with which to bargain. Your daughter might also be reminded of the other expenses that are sometimes imposed by sexual irresponsibility, including those associated with venereal disease, unwanted pregnancies, and fatherless children. By contrast, the biblical concept of morality offers overwhelming advantages for a woman, even if the matter of right and wrong were of no significance. Through moral behavior she is more likely to achieve self-respect, the respect of society, the love of a husband, and provision for the needs of her children. The current move toward common-law marriages (unmarried couples living as man and wife) offers no legal protection and no security to the "wife" involved. Similarly, the new morality is a tragic imposition on the female sex: women satisfy the desires of males while assuming the full responsibilities, risks, and consequences themselves. Then when their youth begins to fade, as inevitably it does, they will find little sympathy from the men who have exploited them.

It would be wise for all girls to understand this message. Parents have the responsibility to lay the facts before their teen-agers in this manner, but the ultimate decision must then rest in their hands.

7. I am the superintendent of a large Sunday school and we're having considerable problems with the control of our young members. If we discipline the children, we might drive them away from the church, and we don't want to lose them. What would you recommend?

I think you should run the risk of losing a few children rather than face the certainty of damaging them all. How can you teach respect for God if you allow chaos to reign in His house? When a child is disruptive in a Sunday school class, he should be taken aside and given a firm message similar to this one: "Lester, you are very welcome at our church, and we want you to enjoy yourself while you're here. But you seem to be having a little trouble cooperating. I want you to know that this is the house of God, and we can't allow you or anyone to be disrespectful here. If you can't be quiet while you're in class, we'll have to ask you to leave. You can come back anytime you decide to participate like the others." If his parents are members of the church, it would be wise to discuss the matter with them, requesting their assistance with the problem. Rather than losing this child, you are more likely to gain his allegiance by demanding respect.

Whether at home, school, or in church, learning is impossible in an atmosphere of disorder. A permissive attitude toward group anarchy is the most certain way to guarantee the failure of your objectives.

8. How do you feel about having a family council, where each member of the family has an equal vote on decisions affecting the entire family?

It's a good idea to let each member of the family know that the others value his viewpoint and opinion. Most important decisions should be shared within the group because that is an excellent way to build fidelity and family loyalty. However, the equal vote idea is carrying the concept too far; an eight-year-old should not have the same influence that his mother and father have in making decisions. It should be clear to everyone that the parents are the benevolent captains of the ship.

9. We've heard a lot about war toys. Do you think they are damaging to children?

Kids have been playing cowboys and Indians and other combat games for hundreds of years, and I'm inclined to feel that the current worry is unfounded. Young boys, particularly, live in a feminine world; they're with their mothers far more than their dads. The teachers of nursery school, kindergarten, and elementary school are likely to be women. Their Sunday school teachers are probably female, too. In this sugar and spice world, I think it is healthy for boys to identify with masculine models, even if the setting involves combat. Two boys can "shoot" each other without emotional arousal. "Bang! Bang! You're dead," they shout.

I do believe parents should limit the amount of violence and killing their children view on television and in the movies. The technology of audio-visual electronics has become tremendously effective, and can be far more stimulating and damaging. Measurable physiological changes occur while a child is watching a violent movie; the pulse rate quickens, eyes dilate, hands sweat, the mouth goes dry, and breathing accelerates. If repeated often, the emotional impact of this experience should be obvious.

10. Does poverty cause crime?

Not directly. If it did, the amount of crime occurring in a country would be parallel to its degree of poverty. America is enjoying its greatest period of sustained affluence in history, yet it is also experiencing a long-term crime wave. Lawlessness is more likely to occur in a society where crime appears to pay; that is, crime thrives where the chances of detection and punishment are thought to be small. When premeditated crime succeeds, it provides tremendous reinforcement for repeat performances. Reportedly, seventy-five percent of large city bank robberies are never solved, which is an encouraging statistic to some men with big materialistic desires but small incomes.

Widespread drug addiction is another certain contributor to the crime rate. "Junkies" often require $100 to $150 per day to support their drug habit. Most of this money is "raised" by stealing anything that isn't nailed down. These are the real causes of crime. Poverty provides a setting in which both of these factors can operate, but the real villain in crime is a poverty of inner morality.

Senator John McClellan, Chairman of the Senate Permanent Subcommittee on Investigations, stated recently that a criminal's chance for being punished for a serious crime is less than one in twenty. Ninety-five percent of the individuals committing serious crimes are either never caught or are acquitted or placed on probation without serving time in prison. It is apparent that we have a "forgive and forget" system of justice — forgive the criminal and forget his victim. Senator McClellan feels, and I certainly agree, that the crime rate will continue to escalate as long as the odds favor the criminal so definitely.

11. My four-year-old frequently comes running home in tears because she has been hit by one of her little friends. I have taught her that it is not right to hit others, but now they are making life miserable for my little girl. What should I do?

I think you were wise to teach your daughter not to hit and hurt others, but self-defense is another matter. Children can be unmerciful in their torment of a defenseless child. When youngsters play together, they each want to have the best toys and determine the ground rules to their own advantage. If they find they can predominate by simply flinging a well-aimed fist at the nose of their playmate, someone is likely to get hit. I'm sure there are those who disagree with me on this issue, but I believe you should teach your child to fight back when attacked.

I recently consulted with a mother who was worried about her small daughter's inability to defend herself. There was one child in their neighborhood who would crack 3-year-old Ann in the face at the slightest provocation. This little bully, named Joan, was very small and feminine, but she never felt the sting of retaliation because Ann had been taught not to fight. I recommended that Ann's mother tell her to hit Joan back if she was hit first. Several days later the mother heard a loud altercation outside, followed by a brief scuffle. Then Joan began crying and went home. Ann walked casually into the house with her hands in her pockets, and explained, "Joan socked me so I had to help her remember not to hit me again." Ann had efficiently returned an eye for an eye and a tooth for a tooth. She and Joan have played together much more peacefully since that time.

Generally speaking, a parent should emphasize the stupidity of fighting. But to force a child to stand passively while being clobbered is to leave him at the mercy of his cold-blooded peers.

12. What place should fear occupy in a child's attitude toward his mother or father?

There is a narrow difference between acceptable, healthy fear and the destructive variety. A child should have a general apprehension about the consequences of attacking his parent. By contrast, he should not lie awake at night worrying about parental aggression or hostility. Perhaps a crude example will illustrate the difference between these aspects of fear. A busy highway can be a dangerous place to take a walk. In fact, it would be suicidal to stroll down the fast lane of a freeway at six P.M. on any Friday. I would not be so foolish as to get my exercise in that manner because I have a healthy fear of fast-moving automobiles. As long as I don't behave ridiculously, I have no cause for alarm. I am unthreatened by this source of danger because it only reacts to my willful defiance. I want my child to view me with the same regard. As long as he does not choose to challenge me, openly and willfully, he lives in total safety. He need not duck and flinch when I suddenly scratch my eyebrow. He should have no fear that I will ridicule him or treat him unkindly. He can enjoy complete security and safety — until he chooses to attack me. Then I'll give him reason to fear. This concept of fear is modeled after God's relationship with man; "Fear of God is the beginning of wisdom," we are taught. He is a God of awesome wrath, and at the same time, a God of infinite love and mercy. These attributes are complementary, and should be represented in lesser degree in our homes.

13. I see now that I've been doing many things wrong with my children. Can I undo the harm?

Once the child reaches adolescence, it is very late to be reversing the trends; before that time, though, you may yet be able to instill the proper attitudes in your child. Fortunately, we are permitted to make a few mistakes with our children. No one can expect to do everything right, and it is not the few errors that destroy a child. It is the consistent influence of conditions throughout childhood.

VI

Discipline Gone to Pot

There is no more certain destroyer of self-discipline and self-control than the abusive use of drugs. The teen-ager who has begun taking narcotics often shows a sudden disinterest in everything that formerly challenged him. His school work is ignored and his hobbies are forgotten. His personal appearance becomes sloppy and dirty. He refuses to carry responsibility and he avoids the activities that would cause him to expend effort. His relationship with his parents deteriorates rapidly and he suddenly terminates many of his lifelong friendships. The young drug user is clearly marching to a new set of drums — and disaster often awaits him at the end of the trail.

During 1967 and early 1968, I served as a consultant for a federal narcotics project in a large metropolitan area. Part of my responsibility was to conduct psychological evaluations for thirty-two former addicts who were being trained to help current users. Even though these ex-addicts had supposedly ended their narcotics habit, each of their lives reflected the immeasurable human tragedy imposed by drug abuse. Several of the men had first been arrested during

their early teens and subsequently circulated in and out of
prison for more than thirty years. Most of them had endured extreme poverty and hardship during their youth.
Each man described his own pathetic childhood, involving
broken homes, parental alcoholism, severe beatings, and
loss of loved ones. The typical example which follows was
taken from the written evaluation of Floyd, a 27-year-old
Caucasian who had spent seventeen years in prison.

In the hour before Floyd's appointment, another
subject was being evaluated, yet Floyd broke into the
room without knocking. It was immediately apparent
that he had interrupted something important, but he
offered no apology. He wore a dirty, stretched T-shirt
and an old Russian hat, and his hair was disheveled.
Later during his testing session, he belched loudly
but offered no comment. He spoke without tact or social grace. The examiner's first reaction was one of irritation and rejection. However, as the testing session
progressed and Floyd's background unfolded, the events
in his childhood so totally explained his present behavior that acceptance and compassion replaced the revul-
sion. Floyd was a child who was hopelessly doomed
by fate. His father was an alcoholic whose drinking
kept the family in utter poverty. Floyd had four sis-
ters, and the family endured the same hardship typically
experienced in impoverished alcoholic homes. But
Floyd's situation worsened significantly when he was
seven years old. His mother departed with another
man, leaving the five children without fanfare or notice.
The children were left in the "care" of their alcoholic
father who was completely unqualified for the responsibility. The needy youngsters were forced to lean on
each other — they had no one else. This situation existed through the remainder of Floyd's childhood and
adolescence. He had no guidance, no religious training,
no social instruction, and no love. He bears the deep
psychological scars from the lack of parental concern.

He has grown like a wild weed — uncultivated, undisciplined, and unappreciated.

When he entered school, Floyd felt dirty, ragged, and inadequate. He had few friends and he fought regularly. To compound matters, he developed a difficult reading problem. Consequently, he felt foolish and out of place in school. All through the elementary and junior high school years he experienced the daily ego assaults of school failure and social ridicule. He hated high school even more intensely. When he reached the legal dropout age, he immediately quit school. It is not surprising that narcotics and lawlessness appealed to him.

Another man in the project, named Phil, described his experience with heroin — the most dangerous of all drugs and the one which is now being used by teen-agers in epidemic proportions.

I was arrested for stealing a car when I was thirteen and sent to a reform school until I was fourteen. I got hooked on heroin right away and my parents kicked me out of the house; I've been on my own ever since. One year later I was arrested again and sent off for two and one-half years. When I was released I was immediately involved in all kinds of burglaries, including a pharmacy robbery. I was arrested for that offense and put in prison for another year, and I was free only a few hours before I was back on heroin again. I was out of prison for three weeks and then sent back for another term. This cycle went on for fourteen years. I've now been out only five months, but this is the first time I've stayed clean.

I was hooked worse after the last time I was released. I had an unending supply of heroin because I was selling the stuff. By that time I had a common law relationship with a girl, and she built up the same habit. She worked as a prostitute to make enough money to support her habit. It was costing us $20.00 each just to go

to sleep at night. Every five hours we had to have a fix.
We were stealing everything that wasn't nailed down.
We were always sick. We started leaning on each other, telling each other that "it's going to be all right."
For the first time in my life I felt something for some-
body else; I let the barricade down for the first time. I
let myself care for someone. Then we were arrested for
armed robbery and forced to go through withdrawal
symptoms. I took the kick episode terribly. I was so
badly hooked that I hemorrhaged inside. My wife tried
to commit suicide. We were both delirious. The first
thing I remember is the doctor yelling at me, "You're
going to die, you're going to die — who's your next of
kin?" I can't remember anything more. I made up my
mind, however, that I wasn't going to die. I began to
recuperate and I did much thinking. After I got out of
prison this last May I found my common law wife again
and she had started using narcotics again. I told her to
stop or forget it this time. She would not give up her
heroin and so our relationship ended. It caused me
great emotional pain to cut her out of my life. She's in
San Francisco now; she just got out of prison and I'm
sure she's using heroin again.

Examiner: Do you have any regrets?
Phil: Drugs were my means of survival.

While it is not surprising that Floyd and Phil turned to
narcotics as a convenient escape from their difficulties, the
motivation of many affluent teen-agers is much less apparent. It is not unusual for a middle or upper class adolescent to become addicted to harmful drugs, even though he
lived in a home where love and goodness abounded. This
tragedy occurs at all levels of society; no child is immune to
the threat — neither yours nor mine. Every parent must
inform himself of the facts regarding drug abuse. We should
be able to recognize its symptoms and stand prepared to

guide our children should the need arise. The remainder of this chapter is devoted to a brief review of the essential information parents should know about narcotics and drug abuse. Though some of the facts are technical, it is recommended that the reader learn or even memorize the important details from this summary.

WHAT ARE THE SYMPTOMS OF DRUG ABUSE?

At the beginning of this chapter I mentioned several of the attitudinal and behavioral characteristics of individuals who are using harmful drugs. Listed below are eight related physical and emotional symptoms that may indicate drug abuse by your child.

1. Inflammation of the eyelids and nose is common. The pupils of the eyes are either very wide or very small, depending on the kind of drugs internalized.
2. The extremes of energy may be represented. Either the individual is sluggish, gloomy, and withdrawn, or he may be loud, hysterical, and jumpy.
3. The appetite is extreme — either very great or very poor. Weight loss may occur.
4. The personality suddenly changes; the individual may become irritable, inattentive, and confused, or aggressive, suspicious, and explosive.
5. Body and breath odor is often bad. Cleanliness is generally ignored.
6. The digestive system may be upset — diarrhea, nausea, and vomiting may occur. Headaches and double vision are also common. Other signs of physical deterioration may include change in skin tone and body stance.
7. Needle marks on the body, usually appearing on the arms, are an important symptom. These punctures sometimes get infected and appear as sores and boils.

8. Moral values often crumble and are replaced by new, way-out ideas and values.

Each drug produces its own unique symptoms; thus, the above list is not specific to a particular substance. If the parent suspects that his teen-ager is using narcotics or dangerous drugs, it is suggested that the family physician be consulted immediately.

WHERE ARE THE DRUGS OBTAINED?

Illicit drugs are surprisingly easy to obtain by adolescents. The family medicine cabinet usually offers a handy stockpile of prescription drugs, cough medicines, tranquilizers, sleeping pills, reducing aids, and pain killers. Furthermore, a physician can be tricked into prescribing the desired drugs; a reasonably intelligent person can learn from a medical text the symptoms of diseases which are usually treated with the drug he wants. Prescriptions can also be forged and passed at local pharmacies. Some drugs reach the "street market" after having been stolen from pharmacies, doctors' offices or manufacturers' warehouses. However, the vast majority of drugs are smuggled into this country — perhaps after being manufactured here and sold abroad. It is estimated that eight billion doses of dangerous drugs are manufactured annually in the United States, and approximately half of these reach the black market.

HOW MUCH DO NARCOTICS COST?

Though the prices of various illicit drugs vary, the following figures represent the approximate black market values for the substances indicated at the present time:

1. Amphetamines: 10 cents per pill.
2. Methamphetamine: $3.00 to $5.00 per small paper package (one injection).
3. Barbiturates: 20 cents per pill.
4. Marijuana cigarettes: 50 cents each.
5. Heroin: $2.50 to $5.00 per capsule (one injection). Within a few months time, the cost of heroin usage can range from $20.00 to $200.00 a day.

WHY DO THE KIDS DO IT?

If we are to help adolescents avoid the tragedy of drug abuse, we must understand the typical circumstances surrounding initial decisions to experiment with narcotics. It is not generally true that unscrupulous "pushers" give teen-agers their first dose. Rather, the introduction to drug usage is usually made from friend to friend in a social atmosphere. Marijuana and pills are frequently distributed at parties where a nonuser cannot refuse to participate without appearing square and unsophisticated. Many teen-agers would literally risk their lives if they thought their peer group demanded them to do so, and this need for social approval is instrumental in the initiation of most drug habits.

The article that follows, titled "Your Friend, Bill," offers an explicit description of how an unwitting teen-ager can innocently fall into the drug trap. It was written by John W. Carpenter, Chief of Police in Carpinteria, California, and was first published in the *FBI Law Enforcement Bulletin,* February, 1970. Both Chief Carpenter and FBI Director J. Edgar Hoover gave their permission for the article to be reprinted here.

"YOUR FRIEND, BILL"

Introduction

After many years of working narcotics investigations and talking with addicts, a police officer can recognize a common pattern which develops among drug users. It is easy to predict where most individuals will end up through narcotics use and what steps they will take to get there. The beginning experimentation, the psychological and physiological effects, and the user's conduct are as easy to follow as a roadmap. What is not predictable is just how far the journey will go before the traveler turns down the dead-end street.

This fictional story is intended to be a vicarious journey down the narcotics trail. Hopefully, after having traveled this way, the reader will never want to experience it in real life. It should be understood, of course, that the sequence of events described in this article does not necessarily depict the path followed by all persons who ever "popped" a pill or experimented with marijuana or even those who became drug addicts. The purpose here is to show what can, and frequently does, happen when a person tries drugs for "the thrill." The risk of becoming "hooked" is too great, and once you are hooked, as most addicts will tell you, it is too late.

The victim of our story is just a plain, ordinary, 16-year-old youth. He is not a top student, but he is a good student. He enjoys sports as a spectator, and his homelife in a "middle class" neighborhood is average. In short, he is like your son or mine, except that he has a friend named "Bill."

Narrative

Remember your first real introduction to narcotics?

I do not mean just talking about it as you did in school or the occasional magazine article you read. These are far away and unreal. Many times, the topic of drugs was handled in a light vein by friends and even by some of your teachers. And remember the one teacher who told your class, "Be individualists; make up your own mind about marijuana."

Well, you had no intention of using marijuana, but the red capsule Bill gave you at the basketball game was different. Surely, only one pill would be harmless, and besides it looked similar to those the doctor prescribed when you were sick. Bill was your best friend. He wouldn't do anything to hurt you, but still you didn't take it when he gave it to you. Later, your mother went out for the afternoon, and you were alone. Why not try it just one time? Remember, that as you swallowed the red capsule with a glass of water, you felt a kind of excitement, not from a capsule, but because you were doing something you knew was wrong.

Pretty soon, however, you did feel the effects of the capsule that Bill called a "Red" and you recognized it from a chart as a secobarbital sodium capsule. There was a nice, warm, comfortable feeling in your stomach and you seemed relaxed all over. You suddenly felt that the world was a great place and any problems or fears were now gone. You felt sleepy, but it would have been a shame to waste that nice feeling on sleep.

And then remember how you thought of your dad and how each night when he got home he had a cocktail and stretched out in a big chair and relaxed? Could it be that he felt the same thing you were experiencing then? Before you could ponder that question any further, sleep took over, and your last thought was that anything which made you feel so good could not be bad.

Everyone Was Doing It

The second turning point in your life came two days later, when you asked Bill if he had another "Red" you could have. Remember, Bill offered you the first one, but this time you asked him for one. And Bill, being your best friend, gave you three capsules. You did a lot of rationalizing during that period. You were not out fooling around and getting into trouble like so many kids. Sure, you were taking "Reds" occasionally, some you bought from Bill, but it was at home and it made you relax and feel so much better. Yours was an entirely different situation than others you had heard about; besides, everyone was doing it.

Then you had your first disappointment. You went to Bill to buy some more "Reds" and he did not have any. It was a letdown to think that you were not going to experience that warm glow again. Bill was quick to tell you that, although he had no "Reds," he had some "Whites." You later found out that "Whites" were benzedrine, also known as "Bennies." He also told you that this was an "up," whereas the "Reds" were a "down." This did not mean much at the time, but when you took your first "Bennie," you found out.

You suddenly felt full of energy and good all over. Where the "Red" made you feel sleepy and slow, this pill made you wide awake and full of life. You even made your mother happy when you went home, mowed the lawn, trimmed the hedge, and put out the trash without being asked. That is when she told you that she was glad to see you acting that way because she had been worrying lately because you always seemed to be sleepy and tired.

From User to Seller

But what happened that night? Because Benzedrine is a stimulant, you could not sleep. You rolled and tossed for hours, remember? At one point you even thought about sneaking out of the house to see if you could go find someone with some "Reds." You knew that would let you sleep. But there was too much danger of waking your mom and dad. You lay awake all night.

Do you recall how you laughed at your mother the next morning when she said you looked tired and suggested that maybe you worked too hard the day before? At any rate, you were smart enough to realize that "Bennies" were not your bag.

And it was easy to slip from user to seller. Bill told you that he would sell you twenty "Reds" for the price of ten. You could then sell the ten, make back your money, and have your fun for free. It was not the money that mattered; your mom always saw that you had plenty. It was the feeling of being important, of having other kids ask for you; and it seemed many of the kids looked up to you.

Bill had introduced you to his "connection" by this time, so that you could buy your own "Reds." You were buying fifty at a time. You were not using nearly that many, but other people were depending on you for their supply. You did notice about this time, with a passing thought, that your "Reds" were not giving you the same feeling they did before. They probably were not as strong as the first ones you had. This was no great problem; it just meant you had to take a few more for that good feeling.

About this time, two new things came to your attention. The first was that you seemed to be having a lot of trouble in school. Your grades started dropping and notes were sent home to your folks. This did not bother you much because you were in your last year and school really seemed to be a drag. It was no longer fun. And besides, Bill had quit school and you were thinking about doing the same.

The second thing was an awareness of the police that you

never had before. Your dad always told you they were
your friends and they had an important job to do. But now
it seemed they always were looking at you, and, occasionally,
when you were with your friends, they stopped and asked
you questions. Remember how you told that cop off one day
when he suggested to you that you should be more careful
in the selection of your friends? You did not care if your
father did like cops, you were an individual and had the
right to have your own ideas and values.

A Marijuana Trip

Besides, because the police had arrested two of your
friends for being under the influence of drugs, they obviously were your enemy. This worried you, too. What if they
caught you when you had a load of "Reds" in your pocket?
Bill and his friends told you that if you were ever arrested,
not to say anything. They said the courts have seen how
the police work and have restricted them. In fact, Bill said
if a policeman knows you have a pocketful of pills, he cannot search or arrest you without probable cause. "As long as
you play it cool," Bill added, "they cannot touch you."

This fear and other pressures made you a receptive subject the day Bill and his friends asked you to go smoke
pot with them. You originally said you would never try it,
but you had handled the pills okay and you were sure you
could take or leave marijuana the same way.

Besides, there had been all kinds of newspaper articles
and television interviews with people, including college professors, who said marijuana was harmless. Anyway, you
were only going to try it once.

Everyone met at Bill's house. You did not think much of
Bill's two friends, Al and Johnny. You knew they had been
in considerable trouble and had bad reputations at school,

but you were there with Bill and you would not let his friends affect you.

Al pulled a small waxpaper-wrapped package out of his sock and unrolled it on the coffee table. There, for the first time, you saw what marijuana cigarettes look like and questioned why there were eight cigarettes. Al said that sometimes one "joint" did not get you "high" enough, so you smoke two of them.

Johnny picked up one of the joints and started to light it. He laid a box of wooden matches on the table. Because marijuana is difficult to light and does not burn like a regular cigarette, it usually takes several matches. Bill jumped up, told Johnny to hold it, and ran over to open the living room windows. He said the last time they smoked pot at his home his mother asked him what the strange odor was. She also saw the matches in the ashtray and asked who had been smoking. The windows were opened, and you were ready for the "big moment."

Bill explained that you first light the end of the joint, then cup it in your hands, let all of the air out of your lungs, put the cigarette in your mouth, and inhale all the smoke you can hold. Hold your breath and keep the smoke in your lungs as long as you can. Do you remember you were not too happy about this because you and your folks had discussed smoking, and you firmly believed it was bad for your health, so you let your breath out quicker than anyone else? This concern rapidly faded, however, for the euphoric feeling hit you almost at once. You felt lightheaded and slightly dizzy, and as this feeling increased, you felt light all over as if you could float. You then took a much longer drag on the cigarette without even considering the danger of smoking.

It seemed like the hands of the clock had stopped and

time stood still. Do you recall how the recorded music seemed so much sharper, and you laughed when Bill described it as hearing in technicolor, wide screen and 3-D, all rolled into one? When you got up to get a drink of water, it seemed like you were ten feet tall and you instinctively ducked as you went through the kitchen door. You felt as if you were walking in slow motion, and when you took a step, your feet appeared to be four feet off the floor. Everyone else was just sitting around the room laughing. Everything was funny.

You do not really recall how long you stayed there. You lost all track of time, but all good things must come to an end. Finally, you started coming down. Remember how your feet and legs started feeling heavy while the top half of your body still felt light?

As you walked home that afternoon, you had mixed emotions. You felt some guilt because you had done something wrong, but at the same time you were proud that Bill's friends had accepted you. Also, marijuana was not as bad as you had heard. In fact, you thought it was real great.

Emotional Conflicts

From that point on your life really changed. You were spending more and more time with Bill and his friends.

You and your folks had always been close, but now there was instant friction. If they were not on you about school, it was your friends, or the hours you were keeping, or your appearance. You knew from classes at school that growing up sometimes creates emotional conflicts in young people and you chose to think this was your problem. The thought occurred to you that maybe your use of pills or marijuana was part of the problem, but you quickly dismissed that thought. If it were not for being able to relax once in a while by smoking pot with the fellows, things would be worse.

Time went on; life continued. Bill made the same deal with the marijuana that he had with the "Reds." You would buy the marijuana cigarettes at one price and sell them at another.

You assured yourself that since you were only selling to your friends it could not be called dope-peddling. You still enjoyed the feeling of importance when these people looked or asked for you. It was very apparent by this time that you were traveling in different circles. Most of your old friends stopped coming around and others never returned your phone calls. This was just another part of growing up, you said to yourself, but you knew better.

Then one day Bill called you. He seemed to be very successful lately, even had his own apartment, and now he wanted you to come over for a party. He said he wanted to show you something. You were glad to hear from Bill; pressure had been building lately and you were ready for a blast. You were lucky to have a friend like Bill who thought of you when he was planning a party.

Bill's apartment was not really what you expected. It was run down and in a poor part of town, but, nevertheless, it was his own place.

When Bill asked you in, you saw Al and Johnny sitting on a couch with two other guys. You thought it rather funny that Bill did not introduce you to them, but it made no difference, you were there for a good time.

Do you remember your startled feeling when you asked Bill who had the pot and he said no one? It was not going to be a pot party. He said he had some "smack," you know, "horse," H, or heroin. Your first thought was to run to the door and get out of there as fast as you could. Sure, you had used pills and marijuana, but heroin was something else. You were surprised when you told Bill you did not want any and he said, "Okay, just watch."

Bill pulled a small cloth-wrapped package out of his shirt pocket. When it was unfolded on the table, you saw a spoon with a bent handle. The spoon was all smoked and black on the bottom.

There were also a small syringe, a needle, and some cotton. Bill explained that this was called a "hype kit" or "outfit." Bill went into the bathroom and drew water into the syringe. He then laid several very small capsules on the table which he explained were "number 5 caps." One of the caps was emptied into the spoon and Bill then squeezed the water from the syringe into the spoon. The handle of the spoon was bent or curled so that it sat upright on the table while he was putting the contents of the capsule into it. The whitish powder just floated on top of the water until Bill lit a match and held it under the spoon. In a matter of seconds, the powder dissolved and disappeared. He then took a small cotton ball and dropped it into the liquid. He said this was to filter out any impurities as a result of "cutting." You thought that this seemed to be a lot of trouble just to have a good time.

The Needle

Bill then took the needlepoint of the syringe and put it into the moist cotton ball that had sunk to the bottom of the spoon; he drew all the contents of the spoon back into the syringe.

As you watched, Bill straightened out his arm and clenched his fist which caused the blood vessels and veins to stick out. He then pushed the needle into the raised vein causing a small amount of blood to appear. Emptying the needle into his arm, he removed it, sat back in his chair, and relaxed. One by one, all the other guys went through the same procedure. Bill got up and stretched out on the couch. The others lay on the floor, and shortly everyone was asleep. It seemed to be a funny way to have a party, you thought, and got up and went home.

You had not heard from Bill in a couple of days, but he had been on your mind. You could not stop thinking about what you had seen, and you wondered what it would feel like to try it just once. Heroin is powerful stuff and you would never want to get "hooked" on it, but you also knew that you could not get hooked trying it just once.

Later, you just happened to drop in on Bill. You had no intention of trying anything, you just wanted to see Bill. The fact that his other friends were not there made a difference, and when he asked if you wanted to "shoot up," you were excited and anxious to say yes. You assured Bill that you were only interested in trying it once, to see what it was like, and Bill shook his head in agreement.

As Bill repeated the preparation process, you were filled with mixed emotions. Again, you knew what you were doing was wrong, but you were still excited about it. You knew the needle would hurt but you were eager to feel it.

Bill asked if you wanted him to "fix" you, or did you want to do it yourself? You told him to go ahead. There was a quick, sharp pain. Then you watched the clear liquid flow into your bloodstream.

"Burning in Smack"

The first sensation was that of burning where the needle had been. This feeling continued up your arm and worked its way through your body. It was almost like fire inside your veins; remember how you once heard a guy talk about "burning in smack"? Now you knew what it meant. The

next feeling you were aware of was the contents of your
stomach coming up your throat; you just made it to the
bathroom. Bill was quick to tell you that this sometimes
happens the first time and not to worry about it. As you got
up from your knees, you felt like you could float. Instantly,
you were relaxed, and every problem you ever had disappeared. You did not care what time it was, where you
were, or what was happening next. You were "loaded," and
it felt wonderful.

You did not know for sure how long you had slept, but it
was now dark outside and Bill was gone. You walked
home still feeling wonderful that night without a worry in
the world.

In the weeks that followed, problems increased rapidly.
You were suspended from school for excessive absences,
and you and your family had a big fight. Do you recall that
your dad said he could not understand what had happened
to you in the last year? You were a changed person, did
not want to work, had what he called "crummy" friends,
and now you were kicked out of school. He also said you
did not appreciate that he and your mother had always
given you everything you wanted, and your mom just sat
there and cried.

When these depressing situations came up, and they were
getting more frequent, you could always find peace and
quiet with your friend Bill. The visits to his apartment became daily trips. Sure, you were fixing pretty regularly now,
but you did not have to. You could take it or leave it, but
it did help you forget these other problems that people kept
piling on you.

A couple of times Bill asked you if you would deliver
things for him, or pick up some money from someone. You
knew what you were doing, but Bill had been good to you
and you were obligated to him.

Then came the shattering day when you were honest with yourself for the first time in years. You admitted to yourself that narcotics had become very important to you. You had been aware for some time that the heroin you were putting in your arm just was not the same anymore. The good feelings you used to have did not happen very often now. Sure, if you fixed a couple of "caps" at a time, you got the bang you wanted, but that was expensive. You were now spending a lot of money for your "stuff," and Bill was still giving you some free.

It was not just the missing "high" that concerned you, but your "downs" were more frequent now and you did not feel good between fixes.

One More, and Quit

On that particular day, you may remember, you were feeling pretty bad when you went to Bill's to see if you could get a "shot." You were cold and shaking. You had good intentions, you were going to fix just one more time to calm down. Then you were going to quit.

When you got to Bill's apartment, he was not there. You wondered where he was. Didn't he know you were coming over and would want some stuff? Maybe he left some "smack" some place in the apartment. You looked everywhere, but there was none to be found. Now you were shaking, cold and hot at the same time, and perspiring. You were in a panic because you knew you were hooked on heroin.

Just as you were worrying about what would happen if Bill did not come back, he walked through the door as if in answer to your prayers. He was the greatest sight you ever saw, your friend Bill, and you would get straightened out now.

You told Bill that you wanted to "fix big" because this was your last time and you were going to "put it down" from then on. As you were cooking the liquid in the spoon, you were shaking so badly you were spilling the precious fluid, and your quivering hand caused the needle to miss the vein twice before you "hit." You felt the "burn" surging through your system, and within minutes your body returned to what now had become normal. Your thoughts of the moment before, about quitting, were lost in the pleasure of just feeling normal again.

In the following weeks your life was pretty much like that of most other heroin addicts. From the moment you awoke in the morning until you went to bed at night, your complete and total existence was for the sole purpose of shooting heroin in your arm. Love, family, morals, and ethics were now meaningless words. The addict will lie, steal, and cheat his own mother if necessary to get his life's blood — heroin.

The Awful Truth

By this time, your mother was aware of your problem; your frequent periods of sickness and the infected sores on your arms caused by the dirty needles told the story. She tried to keep your secret from your father only because she knew it would kill him if he knew, but a secret like heroin addiction is impossible to keep. Your frantic narcotic-saturated world collapsed with your first arrest. You were lucky there was no more heroin left when the police came crashing through Bill's apartment door. Being under the influence and possession of narcotics paraphernalia are all they can charge you with this time, and you will be out in a few days.

Heroin has become as vital as life itself; now you will have to tolerate life without it. You will begin as before, by getting nervous with cold spells and then hot flashes. Then you will vomit for hours until nothing comes up but blood, and at the same time muscle contractions in your legs and back will cause you to roll on the floor in painful spasms. Your breathing rate, blood pressure, and temperature will fluctuate for several days; and you will have muscle twitching, diarrhea, and burning of the eyes until you will welcome death.

The physical torment will be over in thirty-six hours and is really the easiest part of the ordeal. The mental hunger or psychological addiction is long-lasting and will haunt you for the rest of your life. Because heroin is the staple of an addict's life, you will not eat or sleep properly. The dirty needles, contaminated cotton, and unclean heroin will eventually give you hepatitis as it does nine out of ten addicts. You will go through periods of withdrawal when your heroin is scarce and then overdose when it is plentiful. You will rack up a lifetime of physical abuse on your body in just a few years.

Life will be exciting, running from the police and playing the game of staying alive, and each time you stick that "spike" in your arm, you will wonder if this one is a "hot shot." If it is, you will be dead in minutes.

These are some of the reasons the police officer told your mother that the best thing she can do is just forget she ever had a son.

You have come a long way in two short years. Most other kids your age are laughing and having fun, but not you. There has not been a smile on your face in months and you look so much older than your eighteen years.

It is almost too late to rectify your mistakes. It seems like a long, long time since your conscience pained you when you swallowed that first red capsule Bill gave you. By the way, where is your friend Bill now that you really need a true friend? Oh, that was his body that the police found in an alley last night with a needle in his arm. That was your friend, Bill!

WHAT ARE THE MOST COMMON ILLICIT DRUGS?

Dangerous drugs can be categorized into the five major divisions appearing below. Fundamental details are also presented to allow the parent to learn what his teen-ager probably knows already.

1. *Stimulants* (Uppers): These drugs excite the user, inducing talkativeness, restlessness, and overstimulation. They are commonly called pep pills.
   a. Specific drugs
      (1) Benzedrine (Bennies, whites)
      (2) Dexedrine (dexies, hearts)
      (3) Methamphetamine (speed, meth run)
   b. Psychological and physiological effects of abusive use
      (1) Insomnia
      (2) Loss of appetite
      (3) Dry mouth
      (4) Vomiting
      (5) Diarrhea
      (6) Nausea
      (7) Inhibitions released
      (8) Blurred vision
      (9) Aggressiveness
      (10) Hallucinations and confusion

2. *Depressants* (Barbiturates, Downers): These drugs are used in medicine to relax and induce sleep in the patient. They are commonly called sleeping pills.

a. Specific drugs
  (1) Seconal (red, red devils, pinkies, or pink ladies)
  (2) Nembutal (yellows, yellow jackets)
  (3) Tuinal (rainbows, double trouble)
  (4) Amytal (blues, blue heavens)
b. Psychological and physiological effects of abusive use
  (1) Drowsy confusion and an inability to think clearly
  (2) Lack of coordination
  (3) Lethargic speech
  (4) Defective judgment
  (5) Tremors
  (6) Involuntary movement of the eyes
  (7) Hostility
  (8) More deaths are caused by overdoses of barbiturates than any other drug — often occuring accidentally.

3. *Hallucinogens*: These drugs are capable of provoking changes in sensation, thinking, self-awareness, and emotion.
  a. Specific drug
    (1) Lysergic acid diethylamide tartrate (LSD-25, LSD, acid)
  b. Psychological and physiological effects
    (1) Bizarre psychic experiences with heightened sensitivity to color and other stimuli.
    (2) Psychotic illness occasionally occurs
    (3) Chromosomal breakage may develop
    (4) The psychic phenomena occasionally recur weeks after the last dosage is taken.
    (5) Alterations in time and space perception occur
    (6) Illusions and hallucinations are experienced.

4. *Marijuana*: (Grass, hay, J, pot, joint, tea)
  Marijuana is usually rolled into cigarettes. When smoked, the initial effect is that of a stimulant; however, continued usage will produce drowsiness and unconsciousness. Thus, marijuana is technically classified as a sedative.

Psychological and physiological effects
(1) Pupils of the eye become dilated; the white part of the eye becomes bloodshot.
(2) A loss of time and space orientation
(3) Muscular tremors
(4) Accelerated pulse and heartbreat
(5) Apparent dizziness
(6) Odd behavior
(7) Loss of inhibitions
(8) Delusions
(9) User becomes "psychologically dependent" on marijuana.

5. *Narcotics*: These drugs relieve pain and induce sleep.
a. Specific drug
(1) Heroin (horse, H, Harry, smack)
Heroin is an opiate. It is processed from morphine but it is much stronger. The tolerance for this drug builds up faster than any other opiate and it is therefore more dangerous. Heroin is the most devastating and enslaving drug existing. It is not even used medically in America.
b. Psychological and physiological effects
(1) Heroin is a cerebral, spinal, and respiratory depressant.
(2) The initial reaction is one of euphoria and comfort. This feeling disappears quickly, requiring a larger dose on the next occasion.
(3) Immediately after injecting heroin, the user becomes drowsy. This is called "going on the nod" or "nodding."
(4) Pupils of the eye contract tightly.

GLOSSARY OF NARCOTIC SLANG

Acid_____d-lysergic acid diethylamide (LSD-25)
Acid heads_____Users of LSD
Big John_____Police

Biz	Equipment for injecting drugs
Blue Devils	Amytal
Blue Heavens	Amytal
Blues	Amytal
Boxed	To be in jail
Bread	Money
"C"	Cocaine
Candy	Barbiturates
Champ	Drug abuser who won't reveal his supplier
Cold Turkey	Sudden drug withdrawal
Co-Pilots	Amphetamine Tablets
Croaker	Doctor
Dealer	Drug supplier
Deck	Small packet of narcotics
Dexies	Dexadrine
Dime bag	$10 purchase of narcotics
Double trouble	Tuinal
Establishment	Organized society as we know it today
Fall Out	Lose consciousness from drugs
Fink	Informer
Fix	Injection of narcotics
Flash	Tingling sensation after injection
Flea Powder	Poor quality narcotics
Fresh and sweet	Out of jail
Gay	Homosexual
Goof Balls	Barbiturates
"H"	Heroin
Harry	Heroin
Hay	Marijuana
Hearts	Benzedrine, dexedrine that comes in heart-shaped tablets
Heat	Police
Hit	Purchase drugs in arrest; drag on marijuana cigarette
Hooked	Addicted
Horse	Heroin
Hot	Wanted by police
Hot shot	Fatal dosage
Hype	Narcotic addict

Hype-kit	Equipment for narcotics injection
I'm flush	I have money
I'm holding	I have narcotics, can make a deal
I'm looking	I wish to buy
"J"	Marijuana cigarettes
Joint	Marijuana cigarette
Junk	Narcotics, heroin
Kick	Abandon drug habit
Kit	Paraphernalia for injecting heroin
Mainliner	An addict injecting directly into vein
Manicure	To breakup marijuana for rolling into cigarettes
Mule	One who sells or transports for a regular peddler
Nickel Bag	$5 purchase of narcotics
Outfit	Paraphernalia used to inject heroin: needle, dropper, spoon, etc.
Peaches	Dexedrine: light orange tablet
Pinks	Seconal capsules
Pusher	One who sells narcotics
Rainbows	Tuinal
Rat	Informer
Reader	Prescription
Red Devils	Seconal capsules
Sam	Federal narcotics agents
Scarf a joint	Swallow a marijuana cigarette
Smack	Heroin
Tea	Marijuana
Tore-up	Condition resulting from ingestion of barbiturates and amphetamines simultaneously
Turning tricks	Prostituting
Uppers	Amphetamines
Whites, Whities	Bennies; amphetamine sulfate tablets
Yellow Jacket	Nembutal, a barbiturate capsule
Yellows	Nembutals
Zig Zag	Brand of cigarette paper used to roll marijuana cigarettes

CONCLUSION

Perhaps the most fitting conclusion to this narcotics summary is the following "Psalm of Heroin Addiction," written by a twenty-year-old addict:

Psalm of Heroin Addiction

King heroin is my shepherd, I shall always want.
He maketh me to lie down in the gutters;
He leadeth me beside the troubled waters;
He destroyeth my soul.
He leadeth me in the paths of wickedness for the effort's
    sake.
Yea, I shall walk through the valley of poverty and will
    fear all evil,
For thou, heroin, art with me.
Thy needle and capsule try to comfort me;
Thou strippest the table of groceries in the presence of
    my family;
Thou robbest my head of reason.
My cup of sorrow runneth over.
Surely heroin addiction shall stalk me all the days of
    my life,
And I will dwell in the house of the damned forever.

This typewritten "psalm" was found in a telephone booth by Officer Bill Hepler, Long Beach Police Department. On the back of the card on which it was typed was the following, written in longhand:

Truly this is my psalm. I am a young woman, twenty years of age, and for the past year and one-half I have been wandering down the nightmare alley of the junkies. I want to quit taking dope and I try but I can't.

Jail didn't cure me. Nor did hospitalization help me for long.

The doctor told my family it would have been better and indeed kinder if the person who first got me hooked on dope had taken a gun and blown my brains out, and I wish to God she had. My God, how I do wish it.

Appreciation is expresed to the Los Angeles Police Department for permission to reprint a portion of the material included in this chapter.

VII

A Moment for Mom

As the previous pages have indicated, the responsibilities of effective parenthood are staggeringly heavy at times. Children place great demands on their guardians, as a colleague of mine discovered one morning when he told his three-year-old daughter goodby. "I have to go to work, now," he said. "That's all right, Daddy, I'll forgive you," she tearfully replied. She was willing to overlook his insult just once, but she didn't want him to let it happen again. As this little girl demonstrated, children are terribly dependent on their parents and the task of meeting their needs is a full-time job. It is not uncommon for a mother, particularly, to feel overwhelmed by the complexity of her parental assignment. For each child she raises, she is the primary protector of his health, education, intellect, personality, character, and emotional stability. She must serve as physician, nurse, psychologist, teacher, minister, cook, and policeman. Since she is with the children longer each day than her husband, she is the chief disciplinarian and main giver of security and love. She will not know whether or not she is handling these matters properly until it is too late to change her methodology. Furthermore, Mom's responsibilities extend far beyond her children. She must also meet her obligations to her husband, her church, her relatives, her friends, and in some cases, her employer. Each of these areas demands her best effort, and the conscientious mother often finds herself racing through the day in a breathless attempt to be all things to all people.

Most healthy individuals can tolerate encircling pressures as long as each responsibility can be kept under relative control. Hard work and diligence are personally rewarding, provided anxiety and frustration are kept at a minimum. However, much greater self-control is needed when a threatening problem develops in one of the critical areas. If a child becomes very ill, or marital problems blossom, or mom is unjustly criticized in the neighborhood, then the other routine tasks become more difficult to accomplish. Certainly, there must be occasions in the life of every mother when she looks in the mirror and asks, "How can I make it through this day?" The simple suggestions in the remaining portion of this book are designed to help her answer that exasperated question.

1. Reserve some time for yourself

It is important for a mother to put herself on the priority list, too. At least once a week she should go bowling or shopping, or simply "waste" an occasional afternoon. It is unhealthy for anyone to work all the time, and the entire family will profit from her periodic recreation. Even more important is the protection and maintenance of romance in her marriage. A husband and wife should have a date every week or two, leaving the children at home, and even forgetting them for an evening. If the family finances seemingly prohibit such activities, I suggest that the other expen-

ditures be reexamined. It is my belief that money spent on
"togetherness" will yield many more benefits than an additional piece of furniture or a newer automobile. A woman
finds life much more enjoyable if she knows she is the
sweetheart, and not just the wife, of her husband.

2. *Don't struggle with things you can't change*

The first principle of mental health is to learn to accept
the inevitable. To do otherwise is to run with the brakes
on. Too many people make themselves miserable over insignificant little irritants which should be ignored. In these
cases, happiness and contentment are no more stable than
the weakest link in the chain of circumstances surrounding
their lives. All but one of the conditions in a particular
woman's life might be perfect: she has good health, a good
husband, happy children, plenty of food, warmth and shel-
ter. Nevertheless, she might be terribly unhappy because
she doesn't like her mother-in-law. This one negative element can be allowed to overshadow all the good fortune
surrounding her. Life has enough difficult crises in it without magnifying our troubles during good times, yet happiness is often surrendered for such insignificant causes. I
wonder how many women are miserable today because they
do not have something which either wasn't invented or
wasn't fashionable just fifty years ago. Men and women
should recognize that discontent can become nothing more
than a bad habit — a costly attitude that can rob them of
the pleasure of living.

3. *Don't deal with any big problems late at night*

Fatigue does strange things to human perception. After a
hard day of work, the most simple tasks may appear in-

surmountable. All problems seem more unsolvable at night, and the decisions that are reached then may be more emotional than rational. When husbands and wives discuss finances or other family problems in the wee small hours, they are asking for trouble. Their tolerance to frustration is low, often leading to fights which should never have occurred. Tension and hostility can be avoided by simply delaying important topics until morning. A good night's sleep and a rich cup of coffee can go a long way toward defusing the problem.

4. Try making a list

When the work load gets particularly heavy there is comfort to be found in making a list of the duties to be performed. The advantages of writing down one's responsibilities are threefold: (1) You know you aren't going to forget anything. (2) You can guarantee that the most important jobs will get done first. Thus, if you don't get finished by the end of the day, you will have at least done the items that were most critical. (3) The tasks are crossed off the list as they are completed, leaving a record of what has been accomplished.

5. Seek divine assistance

The concepts of marriage and parenthood were not human inventions. God, in His infinite wisdom, created and ordained the family as the basic unit of procreation and companionship. The solutions to the problems of modern parenthood can be found through the power of prayer and personal appeal to the Great Creator. Even the principles of discipline which I have summarized in this book can hardly be considered new ideas. Most of these recommendations were first written in the Scripture, dating back at least two thousand years to biblical times. Consider the clarity with which the following verses outline the healthy parental attitude toward children:

1. "He (the father) must have proper authority in his own household, and be able to control and command the respect of his children. (For if a man cannot rule in his own house how can he look after the Church of God?)" I Timothy 3:4-5 (Phillips).

This verse acknowledges the fact that respect must be "commanded." It is not a by-product of human nature, but it is inherently related to "control."

2. " 'My son, do not regard lightly the discipline of the Lord, nor lose courage when you are punished by him. For the Lord disciplines him whom he loves," (Note: Discipline and love work hand and hand; one is a function of the other;) "and chastises every son whom he receives.' It is for discipline that you have to endure. God is treating you as sons; for what son is there whom the father does not discipline? If you are left without discipline, in which all have participated, then you are illegitimate children and not sons. Besides this, we have had earthly fathers to discipline us and we respected them." (Note: The relationship between discipline and respect was recognized more than 2,000 years ago.) "For the moment all discipline seems painful rather than pleasant; later it yields the peaceful fruit of righteousness to those who have been trained by it" Hebrews 12:5-9, 11 (RSV).

The purpose of this Scripture is to demonstrate that the parent's relationship with his child should be modeled after God's relationship with man. In its ultimate beauty, that interaction is characterized by abundant love — a love unparalleled in tenderness and mercy. This same love leads the benevolent father to guide, correct — and even bring some pain to the child when it is necessary for his eventual good. I find it difficult to comprehend how this message has been so thoroughly misunderstood during the past twenty years.

3. "Children, the right thing for you to do is to obey your parents as those whom God has set over you. The first commandment to contain a promise was: 'Honour thy father and thy mother that it may be well with thee, and that thou mayest live long on the earth.' Fathers, don't over-correct your children or make it difficult for them to obey the commandment. Bring them up with Christian teaching in Christian discipline" Ephesians 6:1-4 (Phillips).
4. "Foolishness is bound in the heart of a child; but the rod of correction shall drive it far from him" Proverbs 22:15 (KJV).

This recommendation has troubled some people, leading them to claim that the "rod" was not a paddle, but a measuring stick with which to evaluate the child. The following passage was included expressly for those who were confused on that point.

5. "Withhold not correction from the child; for if thou *beatest* him with the rod, he shall not die. Thou shalt beat him with the rod, and shalt deliver his soul from hell" Proverbs 23:13, 14 (KJV).

Certainly, if the "rod" is a measuring stick, you now know what to do with it!

6. "He that spareth his rod hateth his son; but he that loveth him chasteneth him betimes" Proverbs 13:24 (KJV).
7. "The rod and reproof give wisdom; but a child left to himself bringeth his mother to shame" Proverbs 29:15 (KJV).

8. "Correct thy son, and he shall give thee rest; yea, he shall give delight unto thy soul" Proverbs 29:17 (KJV).

From Genesis to Revelation, there is consistent foundation on which to build an effective philosophy of parent-child relationships. It is my belief that we have departed from the standard which was clearly outlined in both the Old and New Testaments, and that deviation is costing us a heavy toll in the form of social turmoil. Self-control, human kindness, respect, and peacefulness can again be manifest in America if we will *dare to discipline* in our homes and schools.

Curriculum Vitae

James C. Dobson Jr. was born on April 21, 1936, in Shreveport, Louisiana. He lives in Arcadia, California, with his wife, the former Shirley Deere, their five-year-old daughter and infant son.

Education:

High School — Bethany High School, Bethany, Oklahoma and San Benito High School, San Benito, Texas
College — Pasadena College, Pasadena, California. B.A. degree in May, 1958. Major: Psychology. Minors: Speech and Education
University — University of Southern California, Los Angeles, California, 1959-1967. Master of Science degree, 1962. Ph.D. in Educational Psychology, April, 1967.
University of California at Los Angeles.
University of California at Berkeley.

Credentials and Licenses:

School Psychometrists Credential, 1962.
School Psychologists Credential, 1964.
Junior High School Teaching Credential, 1961.

General Elementary Teaching Credential, 1965.
Marriage, Family, and Child Counseling License, 1966.
State Certification and License as a Psychologist, 1968.

Society Memberships and Honors:

California Association of School Psychologists and Psychometrists. (Served on research committee.)
California Association of Guidance and Counseling.
California Educational Research and Guidance Association.
California Teachers Association.
American Association on Mental Deficiency.
National Council for Measurement in Education.
Qualified for membership in the Academic Honor Society at Pasadena College, Sigma Phi Mu.
Name appears in 1968 edition of "Outstanding Young Men of America."
Name appears in "Men of Science," 1968.
Name appears in "Two Thousand Men of Achievement," 1969.

Professional Experience:

Teacher of sixth grade, Hudson School District, 1960-1961. Teacher of seventh and eighth grade science and mathematics, Hudson School District, 1961-1962.
Psychometrist and teacher in junior high school, Hudson School District, 1962-1963.
Psychometrist-Counselor at Charter Oak High School, Charter Oak Unified School District, 1963-1964.
School Psychologist and Coordinator of Pupil Personnel Services, Charter Oak Unified School District, 1964-1966.
Psychological Consultant for the Federal Narcotics Symposium, Los Angeles, 1967-1968.
Consulting editor for the *Journal of International Neurosciences Abstracts*.

Present Responsibilities:

> Assistant Professor of Pediatrics (Child Development), University of Southern California School of Medicine, Los Angeles, California.
>
> Director of Behavioral Research, Division of Child Development, Childrens Hospital of Los Angeles.
>
> Director of the "Collaborative Study of Children Treated for Phenylketonuria." This study is being conducted in sixteen major medical centers, located in twelve states. The headquarters for the project is at Childrens Hospital, Los Angeles, and the director serves as administrator for the program. He also wrote a significant portion of the original research design.
>
> Assistant Director, Department of Education, at the American Institute of Family Relations, Los Angeles.
>
> Part time teaching assignments at University of Southern California, Los Angeles, and at Pasadena College, Pasadena, California.

Books and Other Publications:

> "The Concurrent and Congruent Validities of the Wide Range Achievement Test", *Educational and Psychological Measurement,* Vol. 22: Winter, 1962 (Kenneth D. Hopkins, James C. Dobson, and O. A. Oldridge).
>
> "The Reliability and Predictive Validity of the Lee-Clark Reading Readiness Test", *Journal of Developmental Reading,* Vol. VI: Summer, 1963 (James C. Dobson and Kenneth D. Hopkins).
>
> "Cognitive Development and Dietary Therapy in Phenylketonuric Children", *New England Journal of Medicine,* 278: 1142-1144, May 23, 1968 (James Dobson, Richard Koch, Malcolm Williamson, Ronald Spector, William Frankenburg, Margaret O'Flynn, Robert Warner and Frederick Hudson).
>
> "Hospital Screening Programs Aid Identification of PKU", *Hospital Topics,* Vol. 46: June, 1968, p. 111.

(Richard Koch and James Dobson).

Protocol for the Collaborative Study of Children Treated for Phenylketonuria, Childrens Hospital, Los Angeles, November, 1968.

"Provocative Observation in the PKU Collaborative Study," *The New England Journal of Medicine,* May 7, 1970 (James Dobson and Malcolm Williamson).

"Altered Sex Ratio Among Phenylketonuric Infants Ascertained by Screening the Newborn", *The Lancet,* May 2, 1970. (David Yi-Yung Shia and James Dobson).

Graduate Textbook:

Koch, Richard and James Dobson (Ed.), The Mentally Retarded Child and His Family: *A Multidisciplinary Handbook*, Brunner/Mazel, Incorporated, Seattle, Washington, (30 Chapters). Publication date: October 1970.

Chapters in this text authored or co-authored by Dr. Dobson:

  8. "The Origins of Intelligence."
  9. "Neonatal Factors in Causation of Mental Retardation."
 10. "The Multidisciplinary Team: A Comprehensive Program for the Diagnosis and Treatment of the Retarded."
 11. "The Educational Consultant."
 12. "Metabolic Factors in Causation of Mental Retardation."